WE BELONG TOGETHER

The meaning of fellowship

Bruce Milne

InterVarsity Press
Downers Grove
Illinois 60515

© Bruce Milne 1978
First American printing, December 1978, by
InterVarsity Press, with permission
from Universities and Colleges Christian
Fellowship, Leicester, England.

InterVarsity Press is the book-publishing
division of Inter-Varsity Christian Fellowship, a
student movement active on campus at
hundreds of universities, colleges and schools of
nursing. For information about local and
regional activities, write IVCF,
233 Langdon St., Madison, WI 53703.

Distributed in Canada through InterVarsity
Press, 1875 Leslie St., Unit 10,
Don Mills, Ontario M3B 2M5, Canada.

ISBN 0-87784-455-0
Library of Congress Catalog Card
Number: 78-13882

Printed in the United States of America

Preface

'No man is an island.' Whatever truth John Donne's maxim holds for men and women in general there can be no doubting its truth for the Christian in particular. To be a Christian, if it means anything at all, means being gathered out of isolation into the corporate life of the body of Christ. Christian islands simply do not exist! In Christ we belong together. According to Scripture a right relationship to God is to a significant degree a right relationship to God's people. The quality of Christians' relationships with fellow believers, particularly in the local church, is therefore one of the primary indicators of the quality of their relationship to the Lord.

This has always been true of course, but its truth is particularly pertinent at the present time, as the opening chapter attempts to show. Indeed it is the author's conviction that the issues raised in this book are among the most critical facing the church of God today.

A major theological treatment of the subject of fellowship is overdue. This little book has no pretensions to fill the gap. It simply sets itself the task of examining some of the things the Bible has to say about fellowship and exploring some of the ways in which the early Christians gave expression to their sense of belonging together in Christ. In the process it will attempt to show how sharply relevant and yet also how wonderfully encouraging the Bible's teaching is.

The book is based upon a series of articles which appeared

in the Scottish Baptist Magazine during 1971 and 1972. My thanks are due to the then editor, Rev. Douglas Ross, who commissioned the articles, and to the present editor, Rev. Angus McNeil, for permission to use some of that material in this book. My thanks are also due to my wife who typed the manuscript and managed in the process to excise a number of obscurities.

If God should be pleased to use the pages which follow to deepen in any way the fellowship of his people in our time, and thereby to extend his eternal glory, the author will be amply rewarded.

Spurgeon's College,
Whitsun, 1978.

1

Fellowship: an idea whose hour has come

'What is life if you have not life together?'[1] T. S. Eliot's question focuses in a poignant manner the agony and the longing of man in our time. For 'life together' is precisely what man reaches out for in his rapidly shrinking planet, and yet what consistently eludes his grasp.

The situation of contemporary man

Internationally the great power blocks confront one another across the ideological divides where talk of 'détente' makes strange bed-fellow with an accelerating arms race and international spy networks. So-called 'localized' wars break out with horrifying regularity in one after another of the world political theatres. In many parts of the world colour prejudice and racism are rearing their ugly heads. And beyond these divisions lies the one which many political observers see as the most threatening of all, the division between the 'haves' and the 'have nots', the hungry and the fed. 'Life together'? The present reality makes nonsense of it. Nor are future prospects on the international scene particularly rosy with hope.

At the level of immediate social relationships the prospect is hardly more attractive. The political and industrial worlds as seen through the eyes of the media appear to stagger on from confrontation to confrontation, and certainly in many places,

9

particularly in the cities, group antagonism and violence are facts of life. 'Life together'? Not here.

The present sense of social isolation does not, however, stem simply from direct social conflict. The whole tendency of post-war reconstruction has been towards a bureaucratically ordered, structure-conscious society in which economic and technological considerations have dominated all others. In this environment many of the personal, individual factors have dropped out of consideration and truly human social relationships have been rendered increasingly difficult.

Nor is family life sacrosanct. A staggering one in three marriages end in divorce proceedings leaving in their train a legacy of bitterness, remorse and a swelling stream of children who will carry the scars of these marital conflicts throughout their lives.

Of course, one can paint the picture too darkly. Some nations avoid war and experience relative political stability. Some societies enjoy comparative social cohesion. Some marriages are highly successful and much human happiness accrues. But on balance 'life together' can hardly describe the life of contemporary man, nor do present indications hold out hope that the future will see a significant realization of it.

Yet man yearns inconsolably for this reality. According to the Bible man was made for his fellow as well as for God. Life alone was 'not good', even for unfallen Adam. (Gn. 2:17.) We were made to find life as 'life together', with our neighbour as well as with our God, and as a fallen being man still reaches out from the depths of his loneliness for that fulfilment of which his sin has robbed him.

Many of the significant social movements of our time are expressions of this yearning. The youth protest of the sixties was certainly in part an expression of revulsion against the depersonalizing of life in modern technological, bureaucratic western society. For many of the young people concerned, dropping out of the rat race was simply the negative side of a dropping into a new experimental pattern of communal life in which personal factors became once more the paramount consideration. Our regret that these experiments were often marred by drug and sexual abuse ought not to hide the significance of the movement as a whole.

In similar vein does not a large part of the contemporary appeal of Marxism lie precisely here? The appallingly oppressive aspects of Marxist regimes in practice ought not to blind us to the significance of the Marxist ideal of a society of true brotherhood where selfishness and exploitation would be replaced by sharing and mutual concern. However naïve we may find their hope of ever attaining this from the raw material of fallen human nature, the force of this appeal to people in every stratum of society is unmistakable. Ché Guevara has even been cited as claiming 'A true revolutionary is led by great feelings of love.'[2] Surely it is the sense of solidarity in a great corporate enterprise aimed at ultimate social well-being which accounts for much of Marxism's continuing attraction. In the Marxist dream as in the youth counter-culture we can identify projections of man's wistful longing for the 'life together' for which he was made.

Modern man like all his predecessors was made for fellowship with God and his neighbour, and despite the massive contradictions to that destiny caused by sin he cannot altogether suppress his yearning for it. 'Life together', life in fellowship; for this man was made and he cannot forget it.

Of course it is a very long journey indeed from the world of international conflict to the state of relations in our local church. Nor dare we claim that all the problems of our political and social life can be reduced simplistically to the matters which will occupy us in this book. The queues at the unemployment offices will not be dispersed by just a little bit more loving all round!

However, insofar as the biblical idea of fellowship embodies the kind of life-in-community for which man was made and for which he still inconsolably yearns, and insofar as it represents a life-style which reverses the forces of antipathy and antagonism which contribute to so much of man's present agony, fellowship is surely a word to be reckoned with in our day.

The scandal of the church

The contemporary hunger for community ought, on the face of it, to present the church with a major opportunity; for the church embodies the promise of the renewal of man in communion with God and his neighbour. The Graeco-Roman world of the first century was characterized by a sense of isolation and longing for community similar to our own, and there can be no doubt that it was the richness of its communal life which was one of the major attractions of the Christian faith to the pagans of their day. Michael Green says of the early Christians, 'Their community life, though far from perfect, as Christian writers were constantly complaining, was nevertheless sufficiently different and impressive to attract notice, to invite curiosity, and inspire discipleship.'[3]

It is just here that the scandal of the church is so manifest, for if there is anything which can be virtually guaranteed to turn the non-Christian away from the Christian faith in our times it is precisely the church. An actor who played the part of Jesus in a TV production on the life of Christ testified to what the experience of portraying Jesus had meant to him: 'I didn't believe in Christ before I began this part. But I do now; what I've read and experienced and played has had a profound effect upon me. I have not been converted to the church, but I have been convinced of the divinity of the man.'

While this testimony expresses much for which a Christian should take heart, we dare not overlook the words 'I have not been converted to the church'. In other words the actor is careful to distinguish his new-found allegiance to Christ from any implied allegiance to the organized, structured Christian community. This distinction between Christ and the church simply could not have been made in the first century. When due allowance has been made for the different context, the fact that this distinction is so possible today is surely the supreme scandal of the church in our time. For the fact is that many people today are prepared to listen to the Christian message, and are even prepared to consider seriously the claims of Jesus, but they cannot take the church.

Nor can we quietly absolve ourselves by the thought that our 'church' is different. If we belong to Christ we are within his whole body and hence cannot shrug off concern and even responsibility for any who truly belong to him. And even apart from that consideration, this revulsion against the church is part of the climate within which we are all called to bear our Christian witness, and hence it is a stumbling block in the way of very many of those to whom our own witness is directed. Professor Douglas D. Feaver of Lehigh University in a recent symposium notes 'two striking facts about the religious scene'. The first is that 'people are everywhere leaving churches (of every theological hue) not to escape religion but to find it. Secondly, to a degree one could never suspect or predict, they are finding it. From the Jesus freaks to the charismatic house churches, people are seeking and finding Christ outside the churches. And often as not the reason adduced is precisely this; in the churches they have found neither personal piety nor communal concern, neither God nor a brother.'[4]

Michael Griffiths in his book *Cinderella with Amnesia* quotes statistics to show that around the average city church there are '2,000 houses with 10,000 people who could walk to the church within ten to fifteen minutes. You can reckon that there are: 500 households needing a neighbourly hand of friendship; 20 unmarried mothers; 100 elderly housebound people, living alone; 10 discharged prisoners; 100 deprived children; 10 homeless; 100 broken marriages; 20 families in debt; 100 juvenile delinquents who have been before the courts in the last three years; 80 persons in hospital; 80 alcoholics.'[5] And yet with all that human need and misery within walking distance, somehow they never come to the church for help; indeed, for some of them, the church would be just about the last place they would think of coming to. Of course there are many factors which contribute to this situation. Not least there is a devil who blinds their minds, and a fallen human nature due to which they deliberately and perversely resist the light. But can we honestly before God place all the responsibility upon the devil's wiles and people's sin? Again, we may comfort ourselves with the reminder that the church's mandate is to *go* to men and women rather than to wait around for them to take the initiative, and so their failure to come to us ought not to be a matter of overriding concern. But the fact remains that there is an unattractiveness about the average Christian church which, in a world as needy as ours, is nothing less than a scandal. The resolving of this scandal obviously involves many issues which run far beyond the narrow limits of this book. But in discussing the quality of fellowship in our churches and Christian groups we are surely identifying an area of crucial importance for the witness to the gospel in our generation.

The mind of the Spirit

The present scene is not entirely without hope. God has been at work in recent years in a number of ways to confront his people with truths which bear upon the renewal of the corporate life of the churches.

One such has been a fresh recognition of the role and ministry of the layman within the church. The reformers' stress upon the priesthood of all believers which had come to receive little more than lip service for a number of generations has today been brought forcibly again before the mind of the churches.

Writing in 1958 Hendrik Kraemer refers to 'a new outburst of lay-participation and activity, or, at least, a growing concern about it'[6] which he discerns in every part of the world-wide church. Kraemer's book, *A Theology of the Laity*, has itself been a significant factor in developing a 'lay mentality', and on many sides voices are raised in criticism of the artificial and harmful division between clergy and laity which has stultified the growth of many churches.[7]

Another evidence of a new sense of corporateness is the movement of charismatic renewal. Understandably this has provoked a variety of response and many earnest and discerning Christians continue to express considerable reservation

14

concerning it. Yet there are features of the movement which only the most biased could deny are recognizably biblical. In particular, the stress upon the church as a local body of Christ where all the members share their gifts for the common good has unquestionable New Testament authorization. Significantly it is precisely this corporate aspect which has come to the fore in the second, maturer phase of the movement, as Tom Smail acknowledges: 'Concentration on personal religious experiences as such could shut us up in holy huddles where we edify ourselves and seek new sensations, but it is surely significant that today in the second decade of charismatic renewal the key concerns are not with tongues and individual blessing, but with the practical rediscovery of Christian community and what it means to be the body of Christ. It is these factors which give renewal its present shape and purpose.'[8]

Nor are these relatively identifiable trends the only straws in the wind. In many congregations there is also evidence of a less tangible sort in a new sense of fellowship and mutual concern.

All this of course may not amount to very much when set against the entire sweep of national ecclesiastical life, but there may be sufficient evidence for us to ask whether the Spirit of God as he moves among the churches is not at work, quietly but firmly, writing the issue of fellowship on to the agenda of the church of our day.

The teaching of the Word

The primary consideration, however, must not be the challenge and opportunity of the present situation, nor even the form and shape of our experience of God, but the teaching of God's Word in Holy Scripture. At the end of the day the true significance of fellowship is the significance which God gives it in his Word—no more, no less. Its importance derives from the fact that God himself confers importance upon it by speaking of it in the Bible. Thus we require to pose and answer the question—what does fellowship mean, and what place does it hold in Scripture? The remainder of this book is one attempt to answer that question.

These introductory comments, however, have hopefully served to show that in exploring the theme of fellowship we are addressing an area of urgent contemporary significance. We are confronting 'an idea whose hour has come'.

1. T. S. Eliot, 'Choruses from "The Rock"' in *Collected Poems, 1909–62* (Faber, 1974).
2. I owe this quotation and several other insights in this section to a paper by J. R. W. Stott, delivered at the inaugural meeting of the Fellowship of European Evangelical Theologians at Louvain in September 1976.
3. E. M. B. Green, *Evangelism in the Early Church* (Hodder and Stoughton, 1970), pp. 274–275.
4. In C. F. H. Henry (ed.), *Quest for Reality: Christianity and the Counter Culture* (InterVarsity Press, USA, 1973), p. 46.
5. M. C. Griffiths, *Cinderella with Amnesia,* (IVP, 1975) pp. 170–171.
6. H. Kraemer, *A Theology of the Laity* (Lutterworth, 1958), p. 13.
7. See for example, M. Gibbs and T. R. Morton, *God's Frozen People* (Fontana, 1964) and *God's Lively People* (Fontana, 1971); K. Grubb, *A Layman looks at the Church* (Hodder and Stoughton, 1964); Yves M. J. Congar, *Lay People in the Church* (Geoffrey Chapman, 1957); K. Chafin, *Help! I'm a Layman* (Word Books, 1966).
8. T. Smail, *Reflected Glory* (Hodder and Stoughton, 1975), p. 21.

2

Fellowship: why it matters

What does the Bible have to say about fellowship? And, in particular, does it give fellowship the place of importance which we claimed for it in the previous chapter? Three considerations are relevant here.

The corporateness of biblical faith

Biblical religion is not simply a personal, private matter. It concerns not only our vertical relationships with God but also our horizontal relationships with our neighbour. We have already alluded to Genesis 2:18 and God's recognition that Adam even before the fall was not fulfilled without a human partner. This text has primary reference to the propriety and sanctity of marriage within God's good purpose for his creatures, but it is certainly not to be limited to that specific form of relationship. It asserts that the 'good' life which God wills for man is one which involves human community.

This corporateness of God's creative purpose finds immediate echo in his unfolding redemptive purpose. His covenant of grace with Noah (Gn. 9:8) and Abraham (12:1; cf. 15:1ff.; 28:14) both carry us clearly beyond a merely personal, individual relationship to God. For these men relationship to God reaches out and embraces their immediate descendants and even 'all the families of the earth'.

The whole sweep of Old Testament history and experience is in the setting of the story of a *people* and all the variety of God's dealings with them. True, great individuals stand out, and the dimension of personal relationship with God in his grace is not without recognition (Ezk. 18:1-32; Je. 31:29ff.; Dt. 24:16; 2 Ki. 14:6; 2 Ch. 25:4; Pss. 1; 23; 40; 51; 84; *etc.*). But Eichrodt is surely correct when he states, 'Old Testament faith knows nothing in any situation or at any time of a religious individualism which gives a man a private relationship with God unconnected with the community either in its roots, its realisation, or its goal.'[1]

Old Testament religion reflects the corporate stress at another, crucial point: in its Messianic hope. Two of the principal categories referring to the Messiah are the Son of man, and the Servant of the Lord. In both cases the concept hovers between an individual and a corporate understanding. (*e.g.* Dn. 7:13f.; *cf.* verses 22 and 27; Is. 42:1; *cf.* 44:1). Now in the light of New Testament fulfilment we need not hesitate to affirm that these are Messianic passages speaking of the Coming One, the Lord Jesus Christ. Hence the primary thrust of these sections is, in that sense, individual. But we need to recognize that for the Old Testament a Messiah apart from his Messianic people was unthinkable.[2] Thus there is a corporate dimension at the heart of the Old Testament doctrine of redemption as it moves forward to its fulfilment in the work of the coming Redeemer.

The New Testament continues this Old Testament sense of corporateness. Jesus comes for the salvation of a people (Mt. 21; Lk. 1:68f., 77; 2:10, 31). He gathers a group of disciples around him and their number, twelve, corresponding to the number of the tribes in the old Israel, shows them to be in his mind the nucleus of the new Israel, the new people of God whom he will bind to God in the new covenant through his redemptive mission. Jesus makes explicit reference to the 'church' which will arise beyond the climax of his ministry (Mt. 16:18; 18:17), and the terms of his final commission carry an implicit reference to a continuing community of faith and witness (Mt. 28:19f.).

Pentecost itself was an essentially corporate reality (Acts 2:1f.) and from that point onwards the disciples' developing experience is unfolded in corporate terms (*cf.* 2:44–47; 4:32–35; 5:12–16; 6:1–7). As the gospel spread out into the Gentile world, the disciples identified themselves in groups ('churches') in the different centres of population (Acts 13:1; 14:23; 11:26). In Acts 15 James expresses his (and presumably also the whole apostolic company's) understanding of the purpose of God thus: 'to take out of them (the Gentiles) a people for his name' (Acts 15:14), and significantly cites in support Amos 9:11–12 which expresses a common turning to God of a corporate group drawn from among Israel and the Gentiles.

Increasingly the New Testament church saw itself as the true inheritor of the promises to the people of God in the Old Testament. Peter in 1 Peter 2:9 for example cites Exodus 19:5–6 and Deuteronomy 7:6 (*cf.* 10:15) as finding fulfilment in the Christian communities scattered round the Gentile world (*cf.* also Tit. 2:14; Rom. 9:25; 1 Pet. 2:10). Thus the notion of a 'people of God' carries over from the Old Testament to the New Testament and sets the experience of God to which both Testaments bear witness firmly within a corporate context.

Scripture then knows nothing of solitary religion. The salvation it witnesses to is emphatically one which has corporate dimensions. No man can be reconciled to God without being reconciled to the people of God within whom his experience of God's grace immediately sets him. Thus soteriology, the doctrine of salvation, is indissolubly bound up with ecclesiology, the doctrine of the church. The theme of fellowship, raising as it does issues concerning our relationships with our fellow Christians, is therefore a matter of supreme importance and takes us close to the very heart of biblical religion.

The commandment of Jesus

The Christian is a man or woman who through the Spirit has committed life to Jesus Christ. Christians recognize the greatness of what Christ has done for them in bearing their sin at the cross, and thus the overwhelming obligation to live henceforth in obedience to him as Lord and Master of life. The Christian is therefore concerned to know what his Lord wills and desires him to do so that he may express his sense of debt to Christ by a ready obedience to his will. Indeed it is this obedience to his Lord which is the evidence of the disciple's relationship to the Master. 'If you love me, you will keep my commandments. . . . He who has my commandments and keeps them, he it is who loves me. . . . He who does not love me does not keep my words' (Jn. 14:15, 21, 24).

In other words our attitude to Jesus is to be measured by our attitude to his commandments. If we really love him, as against simply saying that we do, then it will be evident by our eager desire to conform our lives to his will, *i.e.* by our obedience to his commandments. Conversely, if we disobey or are unconcerned about the commandments of Jesus, then we simply do not love him no matter what experiences of him we may lay claim to or how loudly we may declare our love for him. Love and obedience are inseparable. Genuine love will invariably affect our will and bend it to obedience.

But what are Jesus' commandments? Obviously all that he taught his disciples which has been recorded in the Gospels falls within this category, and indeed, in a real sense, the whole content of the biblical revelation can also be included, since Jesus as the eternal Word and Wisdom of God is the medium of all God's revelation in Scripture.

However, without wishing to qualify in any way the need to obey the voice of the Lord as he addresses us through *all* of Scripture, we surely ought to be especially sensitive to the commandments which Jesus himself attached particular attention to. When asked concerning the greatest commandment in the Old Testament Jesus identified the commandment to love God with all our being (Dt. 6:4), and coupled with it the command to love our neighbour as ourselves (Lv. 19:18). This second Jesus spoke of as the 'new commandment'. 'A new commandment I give to you, that you love one another; even as I have loved you' (Jn. 13:34; *cf.* 15:12, 17;

1 Jn. 2:7f.; 3:23; 4:21; 2 Jn. 5f.).

Once again we see how crucial the matter of our Christian relationships and fellowship is in the teaching of the Bible. Jesus identifies our love for our fellow Christians as the supreme matter for our attention next to the question of our relationship to God himself. Indeed in John 13:34f. he speaks of this love as the characteristic, distinguishing mark of the Christian community (*cf.* Jn. 17:23).

Clearly then fellowship, and our practice of it, comes very high indeed on Jesus' list of priorities for the Christian life. It is a primary point by which to measure our Christian growth and an index of the degree to which we truly love our Lord and are pleasing him in our lives. The Christian who expresses no concern about his relationships with his fellow Christians betrays a fundamental flaw in his entire Christian profession and proclaims the paucity of his love for the Lord who died for him.

The criterion of judgment

Scripture teaches in a number of places that all men are one day to be judged. God is just. The wrongs of this present life have yet to find their just desert. But they will, for God has 'fixed a day on which he will judge the world in righteousness' (Acts 17:31).

The Bible also speaks of the basis of this judgment to come. In the final analysis it will be in terms of whether or not we have availed ourselves of the mercy of God in Jesus Christ (Acts 17:30f.; Jn. 5:22–29; 3:17f.; 3:36; 1 Thes. 1:10; 2 Thes. 1:8; 2 Tim. 4:8; 1 Pet. 1:8f.; Heb. 9:27f., *etc.*). However, Scripture states clearly that our having received God's mercy is something which will be apparent in our lives. Thus it is also possible to relate the coming judgment to our outward conduct, *i.e.* to our 'works' (*cf.* Rev. 20:12f.; Mt. 7:21–23; Rom. 2:5–11; Mt. 25:31–46).

Among the passages which speak of the coming judgment Jesus' parable in Matthew 25:31–46 is particularly significant. The criterion which distinguishes the 'sheep' from the 'goats' is their attitude towards the 'brethren' of Jesus, *i.e.* his disciples (*cf.* Lk. 10:10f.; Jn. 20:22f.; Acts 13:46). An attitude of concern and loving care for the 'brethren' of Jesus is an indication of a heart which has identified with Christ and his cause. Conversely, to persecute and oppose, or to be careless of the 'brethren', reflects a heart which is opposed to, and turned away from, the Lord who is so identified with his brethren that, as Paul discovered on the Damascus road, to persecute them was in fact to persecute him (Acts 9:5).[3] The Lord's Prayer says something very similar, 'Forgive us our debts, as we also have forgiven our debtors' (Mt. 6:12), and Jesus continues: 'If you forgive men . . . your heavenly Father will also forgive you; but if you do not forgive men . . . neither will your Father forgive your trespasses' (verse 14). This same tie-up between our attitudes to our fellows and God's attitude to us is expressed by John, 'He who does not love his brother whom he has seen, cannot love God whom he has not seen' (1 Jn. 4:20); indeed, 'We know that we have passed out of death into life, because we love the brethren' (3:14).

Let us be quite clear. These scriptures do not teach that our salvation depends upon our ability to love other Christians. That would be self-salvation, a denial of the gospel of salvation by grace alone; we are saved only as we cast ourselves helplessly upon the mercy of God in Christ and his cross. However, the reality of our relationship with him may be assessed, according to these passages, in terms of our relationship to other believers. A true relationship with Christ will mean a new relationship with his people. We cannot be related to Christ without being at the same time related to his body, the church, the universal company of all who are renewed by the Holy Spirit.

Thus the three lines of teaching converge. The corporateness of biblical faith, the commandment of Jesus, and the criterion of judgment all combine in a recognition of the cruciality of this whole business of our relationships with fellow Christians. This is not a matter which we can push to one side. We saw in our first chapter how crucial the question of fellowship is for the church in today's world. In this second chapter we have come to see how critical it is from the perspectives of God's eternal Word. It is high time therefore to come to grips with the biblical teaching on fellowship, and we begin by exploring the meaning of the word.

1. W. Eichrodt, *The Theology of the Old Testament*, II (SCM, 1967), p. 265.
2. *Cf.* G. R. Beasley-Murray, *Baptism in the New Testament* (Macmillan, 1963), pp. 55–60.
3. For this interpretation of the parable see G. E. Ladd, *Theology of the New Testament* (Lutterworth, 1974), pp. 118, 205.

3

Fellowship: what it means

We will take Pentecost as our starting point. Luke refers to the life of the new-born Christian church in this way: 'they devoted themselves to the apostles' teaching and fellowship, to the breaking of bread and the prayers' (Acts 2:42). Fellowship was a marked feature of the Christian church from the very day of its birth. We can therefore with justice speak of fellowship as a 'birth-mark' of the church.

But what does it mean?

Koinōnia: the basis of fellowship

'Fellowship' is a word which is frequently used by Christians. We talk about 'having fellowship' with one another. We speak of sharing in a 'fellowship meeting' or a 'fellowship meal'. In general use in this way fellowship refers to Christian mutual association.

The Greek word translated by 'fellowship' in the New Testament is *koinōnia*. While encompassing the thought of mutual association *koinōnia* has a rather fuller and more precise meaning. It means 'having a share with someone in something'.[1] It is used in secular contexts for a business partnership, *i.e.* a sharing together in a business. It appears in this sense in the New Testament in Luke 5:10 where James and John are described as 'partners', literally 'fellowshippers' (!) with Peter in a fishing business. It is not simply that James and

John are associated with Peter in a general way. It is rather that they are associated with him on the basis of the precise fact that they are partners in a business.

Thus *koinōnia* in its usage in the New Testament normally carries with it a specific reference to the thing which is the basis and ground of the mutual association. Now there is no doubt that when we use the notion of fellowship in Christian contexts the ground of our mutual association is implicit. But *koinōnia* brings it right into the open. It implies a common participation *in Christ*.

We used 'normally' in the previous sentence because even within the New Testament the looser, more general sense of 'mutual association' makes its appearance. In Galatians 2:9 the 'right hand of fellowship' which Peter and John gave to Paul and Barnabas is such an instance, as indeed is the reference in Acts 2:42.[2] Nevertheless *koinōnia* in its narrower meaning is a good point at which to begin because it draws explicit attention to that which lies at the basis of all true Christian fellowship, viz. a common participation in what God has done for us in Christ. It is worth exploring this truth for a while before moving on to examine other aspects of Christian mutual association.

There are two important implications. *Firstly*, the fact that fellowship refers basically to a common participation in God's grace in Christ makes the obvious point which we referred to in chapter two, that relationships with our fellows are inseparable from our relationship with God. In that context we noted that it is not possible to have a true relationship with God without it implying new and true relationships with God's people. Here we make the converse point that we cannot enjoy true relations with God's people until we have a true relationship with God. True fellowship only exists on the basis of repentance and faith in Christ. This has implications for human society at every level. There can finally be no true community except beneath the cross.

It is this truth which is the rock upon which all schemes which attempt to transform human character by changing external factors eventually founder. This is why education without moral transformation will simply produce educated devils in place of foolish ones. You cannot build a new society until you have new people. It is this which is the impasse for Marxism. Social and economic relationships are quite simply *not* the ultimate determinants of character. Thus the revolution only changes the context in which human selfishness and greed find expression.

All this is not to suggest that the Christian can be, or dare be, indifferent to every attempt to improve the human lot, extend education, improve social conditions, or establish greater justice and true freedom. How could he be indifferent when he claims identification with a God who is Creator and Lord of all men and of all life, and who has commanded us to love our neighbour? How could he be indifferent when he claims identification with a Christ who in the days of his flesh fed the hungry and healed the sick and welcomed the outcast? But to grasp this biblical truth is to be delivered from any false and easy optimism and alerted to the inherent limitations of all social and political ideologies which claim to change man's essential nature. True fellowship is possible only on the basis of the cross.

Secondly, the thing which binds us together as Christian people is our common participation in Christ. But if thisi s so then we need to see that this carries with it the far-reaching negative implication that this cancels out all other bases for fellowship. Just as in the matter of our being justified before God we had to learn that all our human works had to give place to Christ's work for us at the cross, so in our fellowship together we have to learn that Christ is the exclusive basis of it (Gal. 3:28). This means that we need to take as our brother every one within the church or local Christian group whom Christ himself has received and not simply those to whom we feel attracted on other grounds.

Other common factors such as a shared outlook, a compatible temperament, common experiences, a shared social background, a common level of intelligence, our belonging to the same sex or age group, are all secondary to the common share we have in Christ. One of the reasons why fellowship in many churches and Christian groups fails to attain to New Testament levels lies precisely here . . . that we permit these other bases of relationship to usurp the place which ought to be reserved for Christ alone. Who does not know of Christians whose allegiance to such groupings within a church outweighs their allegiance to the body as a whole? Thus while a case can certainly be made on strategic grounds for a special activity in a church say for women or young people, these allegiances should never represent our primary loyalty. How many churches have been held back in their work or divided into factions simply because this kind of secondary loyalty has been allowed to become paramount? All these secondary groupings are expendable and relative. The primary issue is our commitment to the whole group with whom we share the final reality of union with Jesus Christ by his Spirit.

This fact also in its way indicates the provisional character of allegiances such as Christian Unions or professional fellowships. They are obviously strategically correct in the work of the kingdom of God, and many owe their introduction to, and growth in, Christian life to them. But they undoubtedly are partly based upon common 'secondary' factors in addition to the factor of a share in Christ. In the Christian Union in a college there is obviously a common age and intelligence factor. In a profession a similar kind of common secondary allegiance is clearly present. These groups can therefore never take the place of the local church in which alone the secondary can truly be seen for what it is, and the opportunity is afforded to express that true and normative form of fellowship in which the common participation in Christ is manifestly paramount.

Sometimes when people fail to identify with the local church following a deep involvement in a group context such as a college Christian Union the real reason is a failure to see the contribution the secondary factor has made. What they are missing in the local church is not simply the 'more spiritual fellowship', it is also the stimulus of comparable intelligences, the security of common social outlooks, *etc.*

We need to recognize that these factors, while manifestly

used by God for our good and growth at certain stages of our Christian lives, are never meant to be our true and final experience of fellowship. That lies for us when we enter upon the full life and ministry of a local Christian congregation, where the secondary 'common allegiances' which we have listed are seen for what they are, viz. secondary, and we learn what it means simply to have fellowship on the basis of our common share in Christ.

Obviously Christian relationships which are buttressed by these secondary factors are frequently more straightforward and easier to achieve. But they can be deceptive and misleading for that very reason. Fellowship in the local church *can* be much harder going, so much so that some Christians, tragically, never really accept the challenge. But fellowship in the local church is the real thing to which Christ calls us to commit ourselves. Failure really to get involved in a local congregation after the somewhat artificial fellowship of our Christian peer group is often a judgment, not so much on the superficial and unspiritual church in question, as on the immaturity and spiritual adolescence of the Christian concerned.

Fellowship on the primary basis of Christ alone is often difficult, as we have remarked, but it is also full of surprises and enrichments. The Christian who never really accepts the challenge is in the end, sadly, robbing himself of spiritual blessing and circumscribing his own growth and ministry for the Lord.

Koinōnia in the Trinity: the wonder of fellowship

The Greek translation of the Old Testament does not use the idea of *koinōnia* as far as man's relationship with God is concerned. This reflects the Old Testament's sense of man's distance from God even within the covenant of grace. This fact alone should cause us to pause. The God who according to the claim of the New Testament enters into *koinōnia* with man is none other than the exalted Lord, the Creator and sovereign Ruler of all things whom we approach with awe and trembling.

The new intimacy which came through the redeeming ministry of Jesus Christ, the eternal Son of God, laid the basis for the New Testament writers to make the daring claim, that sinful men and women can become participants in the very life of God. Paul speaks of our being common participants in Christ (1 Cor. 1:9; 10:16; Phil. 3:10). Elsewhere he speaks of our *koinōnia* in the Holy Spirit (2 Cor. 13:14; Phil. 2:1). The apostle John extends it to participation in the Father also (1 Jn. 1:3, 6f.).

Thus, incredibly, Christians are joint participants in the life of the entire Trinity. In one sense, of course, this would be true by virtue of our being participants in any one Person of the Godhead. In the mystery of the inter-trinitarian life of God the three Persons so co-inhere that to be related to one is to be related to all. It is impressive, however, that the New Testament spells this out in its full terms.

It is difficult to conceive of anything higher or greater being attributed to the work of grace in our lives. That we should be pardoned for our rebellion and guilt before God is wonder enough, but the prodigal is not merely received back into the Father's house, he is given the status of sonship, elevated to the very family circle of Godhead and made participant in the life of the triune God.

Koinōnia in Christ: the shape of fellowship

Our fellowship with God, our sharing together in his life, is due to the sheer miracle of his grace. We are and remain sinful creatures. He is and remains the holy Lord God. Thus our fellowship with God is always on the basis of God's *grace*. While our fellowship with God is, as we have seen, related to every person of the Godhead it must always be explicitly centred in Jesus Christ since it is in Christ that God's grace comes to us again and again. But to share together in Christ has some very significant dimensions according to the New Testament and as we explore these we will be able to fill out the shape and form which our fellowship with God assumes.

The Christ in whom we are common participants through grace is not some static centre of transcendent spiritual power. He is the personal Lord of the Gospel stories. More particularly he is the Christ who has become incarnate, been crucified, and been raised from death; who is now exalted and reigning in the entire universe, and destined to return in glory at the end of the present age. To have fellowship with Christ means to share together in the *whole* Christ, incarnate, crucified, risen, reigning, returning. It means that we have been caught up into union with Christ in the whole sweep of his redemptive mission. It means that we are united with him in his death, resurrection, reign and coming glory. Such is the remarkable claim of passages such as Gal. 2:20; Rom. 6:1ff.; Col. 2:12f.; 2:20; 3:1f.; Eph. 1:3; 2:1, 5–7; 2 Tim. 2:11.

The background here lies in the Old Testament. We have already noted the way in which the Old Testament binds the Messiah to his Messianic people. Thus his action for his people is an action in which he acts as their representative and they are involved in it in his person. He acts for them, and hence they act in and with him. The same thought is present also in the idea of Christ as the second or last Adam (Rom. 5:12ff.; 1 Cor. 15:21ff.). Just as we were 'in' the first Adam and so experience the sorry effects of the fall, so we are 'in' Christ and experience all the glorious effects of his redemption.

Here then is part of what *koinōnia* means. It is basically a common participation in the life of God in Christ, and that in turn implies a common participation in the whole sweep of his redemptive mission. Thus the Christian is a man or woman who has shared in each phase of Christ's saving work. They have died with Christ (Gal. 2:20; Rom. 6:1f.; Col. 2:11f., 20; 2 Tim. 2:11); they have been raised with Christ (Rom. 6:1ff.; Eph. 2:1,6; Col. 3:1; 2:13); they are now reigning with Christ (Eph. 1:3; 2:6; Col. 3:1–3; 2 Tim. 2:11); they will one day share Christ's glory (2 Tim. 2:12; Col. 3:4; Eph. 2:7). As these texts show, Christian baptism is commonly seen as the point at which this 'union with Christ' is supremely focused (Col. 2:12; Rom. 6:3–11; Gal. 3:27).

It needs to be underlined at this point that all we are doing here is unpacking what being a Christian implies. *All of this* is true of *every single Christian in all the world*. To be a Christian means to be united to Christ in faith, and to be united to Christ means to be united to him in each phase of his redemption. This is emphatically *not* something which Christians are required to attain to at some point in Christian life subsequent to their conversion. It is true for every Christian from the very first moment of his fellowship with Christ. Indeed in a deeper sense it has been true of him from all eternity (Eph. 1:4–6, 11f.; Rom. 8:29f.).[3]

Thus we have seen that 'fellowship' means fundamentally a 'common participation in something'. We have seen that in the New Testament this 'something' is nothing less than the very life of the triune God encountered by us by faith in Christ. We have seen that faith in Christ implies being united with him in his whole redemptive mission. In other words Christian fellowship in its widest sense concerns the mutual relationships of those who have a place within the Christian community by virtue of the fact that they have all shared in the death, resurrection, reign and glory of Christ the Lord.

Not surprisingly this has very significant implications for the whole shape and character of Christian fellowship. In particular—

(a) It is a fellowship of the crucified and resurrected

The Christian group, whether it is the local church or a more *ad hoc* company such as a Christian Union in a college or factory, is made up of people who have individually and corporately shared in the death and resurrection of Christ. They died with him on the cross, they rose with him from the tomb. Such is the stark claim of the Bible.

Of course there is impenetrable mystery here. It is obviously difficult to state clearly what exactly this means. How could we have been involved in events which took place centuries before we were born? And yet that is not really a new question for the Christian since he has always depended on Christ's death and resurrection for him as the ground of his salvation. All we are doing here is to add to the basic New Testament affirmation that Christ died and rose 'for me' the additional New Testament affirmation that we died and rose 'with him'. It is true that the notion of something being done 'on our behalf' seems easier to project into the past than something which in some sense involves us personally. Yet in fact the two are really equivalent, for what Christ has done for us in the past is to deal with *our* sins. Anything less than that will leave us unredeemed. So in fact we *are* implying some kind of projecting of ourselves back into the past when we make the simple (!) claim 'Christ died for our sins' (1 Cor. 15:3). And despite the difficulty of understanding quite how this projection takes place no Christian who has known the joy of forgiveness through the cross will doubt its reality. We therefore have already in experience crossed the time divide and entered upon the events of the first Easter. The thought of our 'union with Christ' simply fills out this fact to full New Testament proportions.

But what kind of 'union' with Christ is this? It has sometimes in the history of theology been spoken of as a 'mystical' union. Hesitation has been expressed about this term because mysticism is a notoriously difficult idea to pin down, and also because it can appear to imply that our relationship with Christ is not a clearly moral one. 'Moral union' is therefore probably a better notion since it makes abundantly clear that it is a union with Christ in his death and resurrection which is concerned with moral realities, our sin, his righteousness, and our obligation to live henceforth in obedience to his Word (*cf.* Rom. 6:12ff.).

The local Christian church then is a company of folks who have shared in the death and resurrection of Christ. What does this imply for their relationships with each other, *i.e.* for their fellowship? Apart from anything else this fact ought to inject a clear note of optimism into our consideration. The achieving of real and effective fellowship among Christians is no easy matter. Even where there is basic concord of outlook tensions, strains, and division are a distressingly common experience. We are sometimes tempted to despair. In face of these sombre facts how wonderfully encouraging this New Testament teaching about our union with Christ becomes. For it assures us that these Christian people for all their apparent inability to live together in harmony *really do have* a basic unity. They have all been united with Christ by the same Holy Spirit and all have shared in the death and resurrection of Jesus. The old nature really has been crucified with Christ. 'The new nature, which is being renewed' after the image of its creator (Col. 3:10) really has been put on. There is no ground for final despair.

Putting this another way, the call to live together in love and harmony in Christ is a call to become in practice and in outward life *what we already are* by virtue of our share in Christ's victory. It is a call therefore not to a wearisome struggle to attain a standard which is utterly beyond us, but rather a call to realize more and more in corporate experience a reality which in principle is already ours through God's grace in Jesus Christ. What prospects this affords us of a fellowship free from the insidious, disintegrating effects of our fallen natures! This is precisely how Paul sets out the teaching on fellowship in his letters. In each of them the call to live in fellowship with one another *follows* upon an exposition of the basis of fellowship, our common union with Christ in death and resurrection. Thus Romans 12:3-13 is preceded by Romans 6:1ff.; Galatians 6:1-5 is preceded by 2:20; Ephesians 4:7ff. is preceded by 2:5-6; Colossians 3:8-17 is preceded by 2:12f. and 3:1f. The call to live in fellowship is then a joyous, happy call. It is a call to make real in our Christian relationships that which God has already given us. It is a call to enter together into the triumph of our Lord. It is not law, in the sense that we are concerned with an unaided struggle to reach what is fundamentally alien to us as sinful creatures. It is *gospel*, the good news that in Christ sin and all its powers have been overcome, including that which separates us from our Christian neighbour.

At this point some readers may well feel we are losing touch with reality. Is this not to offer too much and raise false expectations? Certainly we cannot forget what theology refers to as the 'eschatological tension' of the Bible, the recognition that the new age of glory has not yet appeared (see chapter ten). Hence there will always be a gap between our dreams and our experience. We can never know before the Lord returns that life of holiness which we will know then. Equally we can never know here that life of holy fellowship which we will know then. Often we will be discouraged, and the attainment will at times seem so negligible as to be nearly invisible. But we do not lose heart. Ours is not to measure God's Word and promise by the meagre standards of our feeble powers and limited vision. Ours is rather to cling to God's Word and promise in spite of all that stands against us, and allow God's Word to be the standard by which to measure our experience. Let God be God! So we pursue the goal of true fellowship in the unshakable optimism of those who really *have* passed together through death and resurrection with Christ, and who are pressing forward together towards that fullness of fellowship with him and with one another which he is waiting to give us at his coming.

(b) It is a fellowship of the suffering

Should a Christian who is faithful to the Lord enjoy a happy, generally successful and secure life? Yes, we reply, without much hesitation; which only goes to show how deeply we are infected by the spirit of our culture rather than by the witness of God's Word. The plain truth is that the Bible represents the life of faith as a generally hard, unrewarding and even painful experience. Jesus spoke of it in terms of a cross, with all that that implied in the first-century world. Indeed it would not be overstating the case to say that the Bible knows almost nothing of the happy, successful, carefree believer, or if it does, his existence is something of an enigma (Mt. 19:24) explicable only in terms of the mystery of God's grace. Jesus' terms of discipleship are harsh in the extreme (Lk. 14:25–35). Suffering is an essential ingredient of the

Christian life according to the unanimous testimony of the New Testament writings (1 Pet. 4:13; Phil. 1:29; 3:10; 2 Cor. 4:10f., 1:5; Rom. 8:17; Col. 1:24; Rev. 1:9), and so it is not surprising to find Paul speaking of part of the Christian's fellowship with Christ as to 'share (*koinōnia*) his sufferings' (Phil. 3:10). To be united with Christ in his redemptive mission means to be involved in a fellowship of suffering with him.

In Colossians 1:24 Paul goes so far as to say, 'I complete what is lacking in Christ's afflictions.' Despite the language used here we need to make quite clear that there is no thought in Paul's mind of our participation in Christ's suffering in any redemptive sense, *i.e.* as a contribution to our own or others' redemption. Our redemption from sin derives from first to last from what he has done himself for us, and in no sense or degree from anything we may do for him. 'It is finished' was the cry from Calvary and points us to the utter and complete sufficiency of Christ's sacrifice and atonement. We can add nothing to that. To add to it indeed is only to detract from it, for all that we do, even in our highest moments of self-sacrifice, is tinged with the curse of the fall and can only bring judgment upon us.

However, while recognizing the uniqueness of Christ's redemptive suffering we do need to find room for the biblical thought of our suffering with Christ in the course of our Christian experience. The Old Testament notion of the solidarity of the Messiah and his people lies in the background again here,[4] and probably also certain hints in our Lord's teaching of a certain 'measure' of suffering and persecution to be undergone by the church before the close of the age (Mt. 24:6; Mk. 13:8; Lk. 21:9, 24; possibly also Heb. 11:40).[5] The words of Jesus in John 15:18–25 are worth pondering: 'The world hates you . . . if they persecuted me, they will persecute you. . . .'

We have no interest of course in feeding the persecution complex which appears to afflict certain Christian groups at times. 'If possible, so far as it depends upon you, live peaceably. . . ' (Rom. 12:18). Yet Jesus himself is insistent on this point: 'As they persecuted me, they will persecute you; they will follow your teaching as little as they have followed mine' (Jn. 15:20, NEB). The Christian is to expect rejection and opposition. The church is the community of the crucified and must prepare itself to walk the *via dolorosa* and taste the sorrows of Calvary. We are called to fellowship with Christ in his suffering and rejection.

The fact that Christians at least in western society are generally absolved from the need to experience suffering is a matter which raises larger questions than those which concern us in this book. It is particularly significant in the light of the relationship which the Bible establishes between suffering and witness. Indeed in Greek the very word for witness is *martus*. Both history and Scripture confirm Eduard Schweizer's comment, 'It is in suffering that the church is most intensively the church and gives its witness most unequivocally.'[6]

For our more limited purposes we can note that the link between fellowship and suffering says something important about the nature of fellowship. The attaining of true fellowship in any Christian group is a costly business. When due place has been given to the reality of our share in the death and resurrection of Christ, and even where the Spirit of God is enabled to pour out his love in our hearts, and where a genuine attempt is made to practise the various components of fellowship which we will be discussing later, the fact remains that there is a price to pay. True fellowship lies on the further side of a cross. It is the fruit of a suffering in which we learn to die more and more to our own selfish instincts and learn what it means to 'bear about in the body the dying of the Lord Jesus' (2 Cor. 4:10f., AV). True fellowship with our brother is bought with the same price which brought us fellowship with the Lord, the price of pain. You cannot have true fellowship 'on the cheap'. It is not available at some 'bargain counter' of the Spirit. A fellowship which costs nothing is almost invariably also worth nothing. This is not to suggest that the costly self-denial we speak of here is equivalent to all the Bible means by the fellowship of Christ's sufferings. But it is to suggest that this is part of it, and a part which is particularly pertinent to the attaining of true, God-honouring relationships in our churches and Christian groups.

Putting the same point in another way, fellowship in the New Testament sense, *i.e.* a fellowship linked to the suffering of the Lord, is not simply to be equated with the happy, bubbly chumminess which masquerades under the name of fellowship in certain circles. *True* Christian fellowship has a vein of steel in it. It is a fellowship which rises out of the passion of Jesus and something of the costliness and elemental moral reality of the cross will always characterize it.

(c) It is a fellowship of the glorified

To share in Christ means to share each phase of his redemptive movement, his death and resurrection and suffering, and also his exaltation and coming glory. To be involved in one means being involved in all. You cannot have Christ in part. To be united with Christ is to be united with the whole Christ. Thus we may put the title of this section in the past tense, as Paul does in Romans 8:30, with all the defiance of faith. To share in Christ here and now means to be destined to share his eternal glory hereafter.

In John's Gospel this same truth is put in another way when Jesus speaks of eternal life as a present possession of those who believe in him (Jn. 3:16; 3:36; 5:24; 6:40; 11:26; *cf.* 1 Jn. 5:13). The point is that eternal life, the life of glory, has broken into time in the coming and victory of God's Christ, and becomes the possession of all who are united to him by faith; 'glory begun below'. The church is a community of the coming glory, and in its experience of the Holy Spirit has the guarantee of its share in the fullness of that glory which will break forth in unimaginable splendour at the return of the Lord (Eph. 1:13f.; 2 Cor. 1:21f.; 5:5).

So we see again the optimism with which we may approach the subject of fellowship. We do not lose heart even in face of all the set-backs and discouragements both with the attitudes which we find arising again and again within our own hearts, and those we are faced with again and again in others. The building may be shabby and unattractive, progress upon it may be slow and often set back, the raw materials weak and resistant in the builder's hand, and yet, this building will surely stand in all the splendour of God's purpose — a temple reflecting the glory of him who makes it his dwelling by the Spirit (Eph. 2:22).

Just as one day we will surely love our Lord with the fullness of unsinning hearts so we are destined one day to love our fellow believers. As there will come a day of perfecting our fellowship with the Lord so there will surely come a perfecting of our fellowship with his people. In this sphere too he is infallibly destined to 'see the fruit of the travail of his soul and be satisfied' (Is. 53:11).

1. *Cf.* A. R. George, *Communion with God in the New Testament* (Epworth, 1953), pp. 131ff., 169ff.; art. by Hauck in Kittel (ed.), *Theological Wordbook of the New Testament*, III (Eerdmans, 1966), pp. 789–809.
2. George, *op. cit.*, p. 245, suggests 'communion' as a better English equivalent for *koinōnia*, but he admits that no single English equivalent covers the same range of meaning as the Greek term.
3. *Cf.* A. Nygren, *Commentary on Romans* (SCM, 1952), p. 230f.; J. Philip, *Christian Maturity* (Inter-Varsity Press, 1964), p. 18f.
4. E. K. Simpson and F. F. Bruce, *The Epistles to the Ephesians and Colossians* (Marshall, Morgan and Scott, 1957), p. 214f.
5. C. F. D. Moule, *The Epistles of Paul to the Colossians and Philemon*, (Cambridge University Press, 1957), pp. 75–80.
6. E. Schweizer, *Church Order in the New Testament* (SCM, 1961), p. 191.

4

Love:
the heart of the matter

In the last analysis fellowship is all about the attitudes which the members of any local company of Christians express towards each other. No amount of 'fellowship structures' however imaginatively organized, and no amount of biblical exhortation no matter how passionately presented, will produce real fellowship between Christians unless they are accompanied by, or are productive of, a genuine attitude of concern for one another. The name of this attitude is love. Love is really what fellowship is all about. Where there is love for one another there will be fellowship. Without love fellowship is only a word. No adequate study of the biblical teaching on fellowship can therefore avoid a study of love—what it means, and how we can experience it.

Agapē: the meaning of love

When Jesus commands us to love one another as he has loved us (Jn. 13:34f.) the Greek word for love is *agapē*. It is the usual New Testament word for love, and it is a highly significant term. Greek culture had a number of words for love, in particular *erōs*. Although this word sometimes today has rather negative associations as when we refer to erotic influences, in the first-century world *erōs* often referred to a very worthy and exalted form of love. Thus Greek mythology contained many legends of heroic acts of self-sacrifice in the

39

name of love. It is expressed by the hero who exposes himself to fearful hazards to deliver his family from danger, or by the heroine who gives up her life to save the hero. That is *erōs*. There was however one invariable element in *erōs*; it was a love for the worthy. The object of the love was always worthy of the sacrifice made.

In Jesus Christ, however, men encountered a different kind of love. Here was a love for the unworthy, a love that stooped to the worthless and loved those who in themselves had no right to it, or claim upon it. It was a love which was expressed supremely in the cross. *Erōs* did not cover this reality and so the early church had to coin a new word. They turned to *agapē*. Outside the New Testament this term is hardly ever used as a noun and the use of its related verb-form is insignificant.[1] It can thus lay claim to being a uniquely Christian term expressing the unique and wondrous love shown by Jesus. 'Herein is *agapē*, not that we loved God, but that he loved us, and sent his Son to be the propitiation for our sins' (1 Jn. 4:10, AV).[2]

Now it is *this* which Jesus speaks of when he calls upon his followers to show love to each other. 'Love one another *as I have loved you*', *i.e.* we are to have *agapē*-love for one another. The implications of this are profound, and it is here that so often we find ourselves far behind the standards of Scripture. Too often our love within the church or Christian group, if it qualifies for the term love at all, is only at the level of *erōs*; *i.e.* it is a love for the worthy. We love those within our church or group whom we admire and respect. We love those who are our 'sort', who live up to our standards and conform to our norms. In fact, we are often, even at the point which we pride ourselves in ('Well, I get on well with people', 'I have such close fellowship with other Christians', *etc.*), really no better than the tax collectors whom Jesus referred to in the Sermon on the Mount: 'If you love those who love you, what reward have you? Do not even the tax collectors do the same? And if you salute only your brethren, what more are you doing than others? Do not even the Gentiles do the same?' (Mt. 5:46–47). A love for those who are worthy and who come up to our standards is *not* the thing which Jesus refers to in John 13:34 as characterizing the Christian community and distinguishing it from other social groups. It is *agapē*, the love which stoops to others as Christ stooped to us at the cross, which is to be the expression and mark of the disciple community.

Is this not one of the reasons why the non-Christian finds us often so unattractive and 'explicable'? We appear simply as another social club which attracts folks of a certain type. We are the 'goodies' who naturally like each other and respect each other. We are drawn together simply by common interests and outlook. Our mutual attraction is simply, on a different level, the same as that of the sailing club, the working men's club, the gingerbread group, or whatever. It is a love for the worthy. It is a love for equals. It is *erōs* not *agapē*. And so they can 'explain' us, and leave us alone. The missing factor here is *agapē*. It is when the love which we express begins to stoop; when we really begin to *love* those who are unworthy, those who have failed, those who reject our standards, those to whom we are not naturally attracted, it is *then* that the non-Christian begins to take notice.

The love of an Elizabeth Fry for the wretched inmates of English prisons; the love of a Father Damien for the outcast lepers; the love of a William Wilberforce for the helpless slaves; the love of a Mother Teresa for the homeless children of Calcutta; the love of a Frank Wilson for young drug addicts, are supreme expressions of *agapē*-love in action. But of course we need to add to that list of public names the thousand daily instances of *agapē* in the lives of multitudes of 'ordinary' Christian folks in their everyday encounters. It is as the church becomes again a community of *agapē*-love that it will prove the promise of Jesus in John 13:35: 'By this all men will know that you are my disciples.' And we can bracket with that promise the words of the prayer of Jesus in John 17:20f., 'that they may all be one ... that the world may believe'. These words have been applied frequently to large-scale ecumenical contexts, often without due recognition that the real point of impact as far as the unbelieving world is concerned is the local community of Christians and the attitudes of the Christians they meet day by day. When the church shows *agapē*-love in the world, which it can only do if it is experiencing an *agapē*-love in its own inner relationships, then the world will take note and be attracted to the Lord who was the embodiment of this very reality.

This brings us to the crunch question—how can we love like that?

The way of love

Anyone expecting a slick 'three easy steps to *agapē*' treatment will be disappointed. There is no 'easy' way to love. Here however are several things to bear in mind.

(a) Love is a gift

If we find ourselves responding to the Bible's description of love with the feeling, 'That's very difficult', then we are in one sense getting the message very well. But of course in saying it is very difficult to love like that you would be wrong. *Agapē*-love is not difficult at all, it is impossible! It is impossible for fallen men and women consistently to love in the way that God loves us in Jesus Christ. The possibility of our loving like that without the help of God was something which died for us on the day Adam fell. *Agapē*, the kind of love Paul has described in 1 Corinthians 13, is not natural at all. It is supernatural. It is God's gift.

That is why the context of Paul's description is so important. The section in 1 Corinthians 13 occurs in the middle of an exposition of the gifts of the Holy Spirit in the Christian community. The way of love is 'more excellent' than other gifts of the Spirit (1 Cor. 12:31). So *agapē* is for Paul a gift of the Spirit, a manifestation of the life of God in the midst of his people. We will talk about the gifts of the Spirit and their relevance for fellowship in a later chapter. Here we note that the supreme gift is the gift of love. Love is a fruit of the Spirit (Gal. 5:22). In 1 Thessalonians 4:9 Paul can say that as far as love (*agapē*) is concerned, Christians are 'taught by

God' to love one another. In Romans 5:5 he speaks of the love (*agapē*) of God having been 'poured into our hearts through the Holy Spirit' (*cf.* Lk. 7:47; 2 Pet. 1:7; 1 Thes. 4:9). Luther in one place writes of 'faith and love, by which a man is placed between God and his neighbour as a medium which receives from above and gives out again below, and is like a vessel or tube through which the divine blessing flows without intermission to other people.'[3] Thus *agapē* is a gift which God wills to give his people.

This fact is crucial to our experience of this reality. We can hope to experience *agapē* only when we are brought to the position of helpless beggars, who freely acknowledge their helplessness and are ready to cast themselves upon God. *Agapē* in this sense lies on the further side of a willingness to deny ourselves and die to our confidence in our own powers of personality and goodwill. To argue in this way, stressing the supernatural character of *agapē*, does not imply that our natural instincts of personal affection and social concern are to be denied or set aside. The Creator who implanted these capacities within us is not a different God from the Redeemer who imparts the gift of *agapē* through his Spirit. Rather is God's redemptive activity to be seen as cleansing, renewing and at points significantly extending our creaturely abilities. Our insistence upon the supernatural character of *agapē* is intended simply to reflect the insistence of the Bible, that the love which has the quality of Christ's self-giving to us is not natural and lies beyond the limits of our human powers. It is for those who are ready to come in their bankruptcy to God and receive it humbly from his hand. The recognition of this fact, and the spirit of humility and dependence which corresponds to it, is the first step towards any degree of realization of *agapē* in our lives.

The fact that Christian love is supernatural, however, has a positive, hopeful side. For if we *are* Christians then we do already know *something* of this love by virtue of our having been regenerated by the Spirit. We have already experienced the life of the Spirit, and an element of that is *agapē*-love. Further, the God we know is a good God, a loving Father who delights to hear the prayers of his children. Hence 'If you then, who are evil, know how to give good gifts to your children, how much more will the heavenly Father give the Holy Spirit (of love) to those who ask him!' (Lk. 11:13).

(b) 'Grow up'

Since *agapē* is a gift of the Spirit it is inseparable from the other fruits of the Spirit's presence in our lives. Thus the 'how' of our experiencing *agapē* is in principle not different from the 'how' of our experiencing any other aspects of his ministry within and through us. In other words we need to reckon here with the 'normal' means of the Spirit's work in his sanctifying and renewing our lives.

Basic to that 'normal' ministry is the way the Spirit uses the written Word of God. Jesus put it thus: 'Sanctify them in the truth; thy word is truth' (Jn. 17:17). Paul speaks of the function of Scripture—'for teaching, for reproof, for correction, and for training in righteousness, that the man of God may be complete, equipped for every good work' (2 Tim. 3:16–17). The Spirit and the Word are inseparable. The Spirit uses the Word of God in all of his work of conforming us in character and ministry to the pattern of Christ. His producing the fruit of *agapē*-love in his people will therefore always involve this basic means. As we allow his Word to dwell in us, and as we wrestle with its truth and challenge and feed upon its teaching, and above all as we return again to the Lord who is the centre and theme of the Scriptures, so our lives will come more and more under the impact of the living Spirit, and so more and more will *agapē* become a reality in our experience.

(c) 'Be filled'

If *agapē*-love is the gift and fruit of the Spirit's presence in the lives of his people individually, and of the fellowship of his people corporately, then our experience of this reality will be directly related to the degree to which our lives are given up to the control of the Spirit. Ephesians 5:18 summons us to 'Be filled (literally 'go on being filled') with the Spirit.' The word used here for 'fill' is also used in first-century contexts to convey the idea of 'under the control of'. It is a little unfortunate that 'filled' is an essentially impersonal metaphor. It tends to convey the thought of our lives as receptacles and the Spirit as a substance which fills them. It is important to reaffirm that both we and the blessed Spirit are persons. To be filled by the Spirit is simply a vivid way of describing the experience of coming under his control at the centre of our lives.

For some folks, and indeed for all of us at particular times, this can be a critical experience. Thus it may be we have been resisting God's Spirit at some point in our lives and when we repent of that sin it is rather like a log jam which is suddenly released as the jamming log is pulled clear. We may well experience at such a moment a marked sense of spiritual power and blessing. Paul's stress here however is on a continuous experience, an ongoing life of submission to the Spirit. Our lives need to be continually and consciously open to the Spirit. That means confessing and turning away from the sins which 'grieve' him (Eph. 4:30).

These two verses in Ephesians need to be held together. It is as we turn from what grieves him that we are open to his fullness. The things which grieve him include, of course, all our attitudes of lovelessness—jealousy, envy, hatred, spite, malice, anger, wrath, criticism, slander, deceit (Col. 3:8–17; Eph. 4:22–5:2). Thus *agapē*-love is one of the fruits of this 'not grieving', and 'being filled'.

(d) 'See them in Christ'

One of the ways we can improve our attitudes towards other Christians, particularly those whom we find it frankly difficult to love, is by learning to 'see' them in a new way. Only too often the stumbling block in our relationship lies in our seeing them through the wrong pair of spectacles. We see them too naturally, too much in the way the non-Christian world around sees them. We have to learn, and it takes an effort of will on our part, to put off these natural, worldly 'spectacles' and see them through the 'spectacles', or with the eyes, of Christ (*cf.* Phil. 2:29; Rom. 16:2). What does this mean?

It means at least three things. As we go through these it might be a salutary exercise to focus our thought clearly on the specific Christian or Christians whom we find it most difficult to love. Now let the Bible tell us three things about these folks.

(i) *They are those for whom Christ died.* In Romans 14:15 and 1 Corinthians 8:11 this is precisely the argument Paul uses to promote 'walking in love'. It is also implicit in Romans 15:7 where the apostle urges us to 'welcome one another . . . as Christ has welcomed you'. Here we are reminded of the sobering fact that Christ places such value upon that Christian brother and sister, with all their faults and weaknesses and objectionable personality, *etc.*, that he was prepared to suffer the horror of the cross on their behalf. In other words if that person were to be put on sale in God's universe you would have to put the cross of Calvary on the price tag. And if they are so valuable to God, so precious, so worthy of concern and interest to him that he gave himself to the limits of the cross for them, can we not find it in our hearts to begin to do the same?

(ii) *They are those in whom Christ lives.* This was a truth which Paul discovered to his confusion on the way to Damascus (Acts 9). Paul, or Saul as he was then named, was involved in a persecution of the followers of Jesus. The risen Lord himself confronted him on the Damascus highway and addressed to him the disturbing question—'Why are you persecuting *me*?' The point was that, such is the relationship between Christ and his people, in persecuting the people of Christ he persecuted Christ himself. This is also taught in the parable in Matthew 25:31f. which we mentioned earlier. The judgment of our attitudes to Jesus is determined (within the imagery of the parable) by our attitude to his 'brethren'. Thus Christ himself is met in his people and we cannot finally separate our attitudes to them from our attitudes to him.

If we were to reckon with this fact, that in meeting our brother or sister in Christ we are meeting with the Lord who indwells them, would our attitudes of criticism and rejection not become impossible to maintain? Certainly, the indwelling Lord may be difficult to discern and seem almost invisible in some of his 'brethren', but the evidence of his presence will be there if we are prepared really to look for it. And whether or not it is discernible, if they are true Christians, he is there. Surely we can find it in our hearts to love and welcome *him*!

(iii) *They are those through whom Christ will one day reign.* Revelation 22:5 speaks of the saints in the new age sharing the reign of their Lord, and 1 Corinthians 6:3 says we will one day 'judge angels' (*cf.* 2 Tim. 2:12; Mt. 19:28; Lk. 22:29; Rom. 8:17). The people of God are therefore destined to share the dominion of their Lord in that coming age when man will again fulfil the calling of his creator (Gn. 1:28). This is the destiny of even the humblest and weakest child of God. In other words we need to learn to see our fellow Christians not only in the light of what they *are* in Christ here and now but also in the light of what they will be in Christ hereafter. It is a staggering thought that if we could see the Christians whom we now find it so difficult to admire and respect as they are destined to become, we might be strongly tempted to fall down and worship them. In spite of all their present weakness and sin they are determined for a future in the fullness of God's purpose in which they will walk tall with God as moral giants in his renewed world.

This perspective also helps us to put issues which divide and set us against our brethren in a proper context and to see them for the *temporary* things which they are. It helps us to reach past these things to grasp the brother to whom we are bound forever in the eternal purpose of God.

(e) 'Remember to forget'

One of the most frequent causes of a lack of love between Christians, and one of the things which most readily grieves the Spirit of love and mars the fellowship of Christian groups and churches is—too good memories. We remember far too well the wrongs which have been done us in the past. These may be quite trivial—a hasty word, a thoughtless gesture or a confidence broken. Or they may be more substantial—public criticism and opposition, an act of malice affecting ourselves or others to whom we are close. But we *remember* it—how *could* we forget? And so barriers are erected and made all the stronger because we fortify them with our sense of justice. 'After all,' we say, 'he said that, she did that, and it was all so unchristian and sinful and wrong.' How many churches are today split and divided because of events which took place years, sometimes even generations ago? And how the blessed Spirit of God is grieved.

Jesus told one of his parables to meet precisely this situation. In Matthew 18:21 we find Peter having problems with 'his brother'. It is not difficult to guess at the background. Peter has been wronged over some matter and has forgiven the offending party. The wrong has been repeated and Peter, to his great credit as he imagines, has forgiven again. But the brother wrongs him yet again and so Peter seeks out the Lord. 'How many times have I got to forgive this brother of mine . . . as many as seven?' One can catch through the dialogue Peter's strong sense of self-righteousness in it all. But Jesus knocks Peter over with his retort—'I do not say to you seven times, but seventy times seven' (verse 22). And then he tells his parable.

A man owes a king a sum amounting in our currency to something around £5 million. Astonishingly the king calls him in and forgives him completely. The same man goes out from the king and finding a debtor who owes him something over £5 has him thrown into prison without mercy. What vile ingratitude and hardheartedness, we find ourselves saying; but this is the story of us all. We are debtors to God to an extent which exceeds any kind of quantification and of which £5 million is the merest token. Only the cross, and the Bible's reference to eternal judgment, give us any adequate sense of sin's extent and seriousness. Yet in Christ, through faith, the astonishing and impossible becomes fact. God forgives freely, fully and unconditionally. And he forgets. But we go out from God's presence and lay hold of our fellow Christian. We recall the wrong he has done us, which in comparison with the wrong we have done to God is as £5 against £5 million. But we do not forgive, oh no! And we do not forget. Every time we meet them it is there. It separates us. Such ingratitude, such hard heartedness must be 'put away', and even the very memory must be erased, in order to restore true fellowship.

(f) 'Be practical'

'My children,' says John, 'love must not be a matter of words or talk; it must be genuine, and show itself in action' (1 Jn. 3:18, NEB), and we can perhaps hear James saying 'Amen!' (Jas. 2:14–26). One of the surest means of promoting love is to *act* in a loving manner. God's love which is the pattern of our loving (Jn. 13:34—'as I have loved you') didn't stop at talk, as Christmas and Easter bear witness; and nor should ours. The New Testament is full of teaching on the 'practice of love' but our exploration of that will come in a later chapter. First we turn to two other important ingredients of fellowship.

1. G. Kittel (ed.), *Theological Dictionary of the New Testament*, I (Eerdmans, 1964), pp. 36–37; A. Richardson (ed.), *Theological Wordbook of the Bible* (Macmillan, 1966), pp. 133–134; E. Brunner, *Dogmatics* I: *The Christian Doctrine of God* (Lutterworth, 1949), p. 200.
2. To say this is not to ignore the fact that *agapē* is extensively used in the Septuagint, the then current version of the Old Testament in Greek. *Cf. New Bible Dictionary* (IVP, 1962), p. 753.
3. Luther, *WA*, x. I. i, p. 100.

5

Fellowship in the Spirit

We have seen that the heart of the New Testament idea of fellowship lies in the thought of our participating together in the life of God which is extended to us in his grace in Jesus Christ. In the last chapter we tried to explore some of the implications of this New Testament conception of fellowship as a common participation 'in Christ'. In the course of it we noted that our thinking about fellowship had also to be linked to the work of the Holy Spirit. Several of the major references to *koinōnia* in the New Testament speak of our common participation 'in the Spirit' (2 Cor. 13:14; Phil. 2:1). And we have just seen that the *agapē*-love which is the essential expression of true fellowship is something supernatural, a gift of the Holy Spirit. In this chapter we will examine the biblical material which develops the fact that our fellowship is 'in the Spirit'.

This truth is one which receives attention in many services of Christian worship in the words of the benediction with which these services commonly conclude: 'The grace of the Lord Jesus Christ . . . and the fellowship of (or 'in') the Spirit be with you all.' This is of course a direct quotation of the Pauline benediction of 2 Corinthians 13:14. The benediction therefore serves as a constant reminder that the gathering of Christian people in congregational worship is something essentially supernatural. It is an activity which arises out of a common participation in the life of God by his Spirit. It is an activity of the twice-born, those who have been regenerated by the Holy Spirit of God (Ezk. 36:25-37; Jn. 3:3f.; Tit. 3:5; 1 Cor. 6:11).

That fact in itself ought to carry over into our attitude to services of worship. To come to meet with the people of God is in effect to move into the magnetic field of the Holy Spirit, where the powers of heaven impinge upon the powers of earth, where the new age of the eternal kingdom of God intersects the old age of sin and decay. Thus every service of worship, no matter how meagre the number in the congregation or how uninviting and uninspiring the circumstances and setting, is fraught with unlimited possibilities (cf. Heb. 12:18-24). We therefore ought to approach it with anticipation and faith that even here the wind of God may blow and cause the dry bones to pulsate with new life from the dead (Ezk. 37:1-14; the Hebrew word for 'wind' and 'spirit' is the same).

There is however another dimension of biblical teaching as far as the link between the Holy Spirit and Christian fellowship is concerned. The Holy Spirit has a further function. He does not simply create Christian fellowship by regenerating each individual Christian and uniting them together in the life of the one Lord; he also supplies them with his gifts (Rom. 12:1ff.; 1 Cor. 12:1ff.; Eph. 4:4ff.; 1 Pet. 4:10f.). This is an aspect of the Spirit's ministry which is in course of lively discussion at the present time and the reader is referred to some of that literature for a full exposition of the biblical and theological dimensions of this New Testament doctrine. Here we concentrate on the teaching as it relates to our theme of fellowship.

Perhaps the first thing we should note is that the gifts of the Spirit do have a relationship to the creation and development of true Christian fellowship among the people of God, as the New Testament evidence which we will examine in a moment will clearly show. This being so we must surely deplore and repudiate in the name of the one Spirit of God the use of this very doctrine of the gifts of the Spirit to divide and cause radical separation among those who are regenerate and indwelt by the one Holy Spirit. That this very truth which is intended by God to be an important means of our realizing true fellowship and unity should have become in certain instances the basis for bitter wrangling and heated controversy, and worse, the separation of Christians into distinct companies for worship and witness, is surely a scandalous denial of the ministry of the Holy Spirit himself.

It is no doubt the case that in certain instances Christians who wish to give a particular kind of expression to this biblical truth have found themselves opposed and ostracized to a point where they have felt themselves driven to some kind of separation. Even here, however, one always wonders whether the second mile has really been travelled, and whether the resultant division has been entered upon in deep sorrow and regret, and with the explicit and continuing recognition that it is merely a temporary breach, and that at every moment lines are open for reconciliation and reunion. One finds it extremely difficult to find any biblical justification for a separation between truly regenerate men and women on the basis of this kind of issue. Separation *is* a biblical possibility, and even a biblical duty, where the very basis of the faith is at stake, as, for example, in Paul's confrontation with the Judaizers in Galatia (*cf.* Gal. 1:6-9; see chapter nine). In all other cases (*i.e.* where the very basis of the faith is *not* at stake) the Bible's teaching is clear—'(Be) eager to maintain the unity of the Spirit in the bond of peace' (Eph. 4:3). How separation in the name of a particular understanding of the gifts of the Spirit can be the will of God is therefore a great mystery, if by 'God' we mean the God whose mind and will has been made known in Holy Scripture. A God who cannot be squared with the God of the Bible is simply not the God known and confessed in Jesus Christ the Lord. And no degree of special pleading on the basis of spiritual experiences, however persuasive or dramatic, can ever justify a course of action in contradiction to the mind of the Spirit as declared in the written Word. In affirming this we are simply maintaining the truth and self-consistency of God.

The gifts of the Spirit then are to be approached in the context of the deepening of fellowship. Perhaps we can best expound the relevant teaching by posing and answering certain questions.

What is the purpose of the gifts of the Spirit?

Why are they given to the church? What is their function? Scripture points us in two directions. Their first and primary function is to glorify the Lord Jesus Christ. Ephesians 4:8 teaches that the gifts of the Spirit are the gifts of the ascended Lord, the demonstration and vindication of the victory won in his death and resurrection over sin and death and the powers of hell. The gifts of the Spirit are thus the 'spoil' of Christ's conquest (Acts 2:32f.). In sharing them with his people he gives witness to his triumph and draws us into a share in his conquest. One may think here of passages which speak of the Spirit's work in enabling and empowering the church in its witness to the triumph of Christ in the gospel it preaches (Lk. 24:49; Mk. 13:11; Mt. 10:19; Jn. 15:26; Acts 1:8).

Thus the gifts direct us to Christ and set him before us as the glorified and triumphant Lord, the worthy object of all our love and worship and praise. They are tokens of his triumph which bid us in the first instance to look away beyond them to the exalted Lord — 'See the conquering hero comes.' He has conquered sin and death and hell. Our foes lie beneath his wounded feet. He is Lord, hallelujah!

Secondly, however, Scripture indicates a function for the gifts in terms of the growth and development of the body of Christ and the deepening of fellowship between its members (Eph. 4:12; 1 Cor. 12:7; 12:25; 1 Pet. 4:10; Rom. 1:11). Thus the gifts are given 'for building up the body of Christ' (Eph. 4:12). They are 'for the common good' (1 Cor. 12:7 cf. verse 25). The Christian receiving a gift is to 'employ it for one another' (1 Pet. 4:10). In Romans 1:11 Paul speaks of the function of spiritual gifts in 'strengthening' the Romans, in order that 'we may be mutually encouraged by each other's faith, both yours and mine' (verse 12). The gifts are therefore a means whereby the local Christian church is built up in its faith. As each member exercises his gifts the others are strengthened in faith, the whole company is bound more closely together, and its common life and mutual relationships deepened.

This unifying function of the gifts of the Spirit is demonstrated at Pentecost where the many-tongued praise of God can be seen as the reversal of the confusion of tongues at Babel where sin led to the fragmentation of human society and the breakdown of relationship (Gn. 11:1ff.). The Spirit in his ministry seeks to undo the disintegrating effects of the fall. In the church, which is a microcosm of the race, the Spirit strives to reverse the process of division. He is a uniting Spirit, and one means by which he effects this uniting ministry is the gifts of the victorious Lord Jesus which he is pleased to distribute to his people. The gifts are intended therefore to be a bond of unity and hence a means of deepening fellowship.

Who are the gifts for?

They are for every Christian. The New Testament passages which deal with the gifts of the Spirit are unanimous in asserting that every Christian has his gift, or gifts, of the Spirit. They are for *all* of God's people (Rom. 12:3ff.; 1 Cor. 12:7, 11; 1 Pet. 4:10; Eph. 4:7; *cf.* verse 16). The very use of the body as an image of the church (Rom. 12:5) is eloquent in this respect. Each member has a function to fulfil in relation to the proper functioning of the whole (*cf.* 1 Cor. 12:14f.; Eph. 4:11–16). This applies, Paul emphasizes, particularly to those gifts and functions which may seem the most lowly and unattractive from a human viewpoint. They are in fact all the more necessary (1 Cor. 12:22ff.). And the distribution and diversity of the gifts lie in their free assignment by the Spirit himself who gives what he pleases to each one (1 Cor. 12:11).

There is no hint in these crucial passages that the receiving and exercise of a gift of the Spirit is dependent upon a special, definable experience of the Spirit of God subsequent to regeneration. The only reference to this terminology or anything equivalent is in 1 Corinthians 12:13, but there it clearly refers to the universal initiatory experience through which these Corinthian readers had been 'baptized into one body . . . and . . . made to drink of one Spirit'; in other words, to that which constituted these folks as Christians. We need to assert the clear witness of the New Testament that the gifts of the Spirit are part of the Spirit's giving in regeneration and are inseparable from that context.

This is not to deny that certain Christians have entered in a new way into the exercise of significant ministries of the Spirit following upon a critical sense of being grasped and endued with the Spirit, perhaps many years after their regeneration. God must be permitted his freedom here. That he *must* act after this pattern in every Christian, or even in most Christians, however, is quite another matter. There is no scriptural warrant for such a universalization of 'two-stage' experience, and much scriptural teaching against it.[1] When Christians enter at a later stage into a significant new appropriation of their riches in Christ, it needs to be understood as precisely that—a new appropriation of what was always theirs in their union with Christ by the Spirit.

In the teaching of Scripture, therefore, 'Each Christian has his charism (spiritual gift). Each Christian is a charismatic.'[2]

What is the nature of the gifts of the Spirit?

Our starting point in discussing the Spirit's gifts must be the Old Testament. There is extensive reference in the Old Testament to a 'prophetic' gift (1 Sa. 10:10; *cf.* 1 Sa. 19:20; Nu. 11:25; Is. 61:1f.; Ezk. 2:2f.; 3:12). There is reference too to a gift of leadership from the Spirit (Jdg. 3:10; 6:34), and men such as Elisha and Elijah experienced special abilities like healing (1 Ki. 17:17ff.; 2 Ki. 4:32ff.), though there is no explicit reference here to the Spirit (*cf.* also Ex. 35:30–33; 31:1–5).

In the New Testament lists of 'gifts of the Spirit' (Rom. 12:3–8; 1 Cor. 12:4–11; 1 Cor. 12:28; Eph. 4:11–12; 1 Pet.

4:10–11) the most striking feature is sheer variety. Despite attempts to relate and classify them, none of the lists is like another, not even the two within the one chapter of 1 Corinthians 12.[3] In addition, both celibacy and marriage are seen as spiritual gifts (*charismata*; 1 Cor. 7:7). We need to let Paul's comment on the Spirit in this matter have its full sway: 'There are varieties of gifts . . . all . . . inspired by one and the same Spirit, who apportions to each one individually as *he* wills' (1 Cor. 12:4, 11). The Spirit is sovereign and free (2 Cor. 3:17). He is bound only by his primary concerns, the exaltation of the Lord Jesus Christ and the edifying of the church. How he will achieve these ends, and what this will mean in any specific instance for a church or an individual, is at the sole discretion of God who is the Spirit. Inflexibility at this point is one of the supreme mistakes we can make. We need to trust God to bless his people in his own way, and to test all things by the norms and standards of his mind as expressed once and for all in his written Word.

It remains now to bring this biblical teaching into relation to our theme of fellowship. We have already noted the teaching that these gifts *have* an explicit contribution to make to the fellowship of the church; they are 'for the common good'. What precisely does this mean and how does it work out in practice?

(a) Work at it

The fact that the Holy Spirit has given a gift to every Christian which he is to exercise for the mutual good of the fellowship as a whole leads to a quite crucial truth about the New Testament idea of fellowship. Fellowship is not something which is simply given once for all. It is something which must be achieved by the whole body of Christians who comprise the group exercising their total God-given ministries. Fellowship is in this sense something dynamic rather than static. Fellowship is something which has to be worked *for* as well as worked *from*. It cannot be taken for granted on the basis of past experience. It needs to be attained ever and again by the renewed commitment of each to the good of all, using the gifts which God has given to each one. Every local church faces the challenge to achieve a deep and God-honouring fellowship in its 'life together'. And it can do this only as each member accepts the call to find, and then fulfil his particular ministry 'for the common good'.

Christian fellowship, then, is a matter of complementarity rather than uniformity. In other words, true fellowship does not lie in all being and doing the same thing. It lies in each being and doing his own thing (though of course we are talking here of what is not his own thing at all but 'God's thing') and contributing it to the whole. In this sense one of the best pictures of God's universal purpose for his people lies in Christian marriage. Here is an ideal of unity, but a unity which arises out of, and finds its strength precisely in, the fact that the two partners to the marriage are *not* the same, but in their very differences complement each other (*cf.* Gn. 2:24f.; Eph. 5:21ff.; 1 Pet. 3:1f.). The thought of the church as the interrelated 'body' of Christ (1 Cor. 12:27) also expresses perfectly the complementary and mutual contribution of each member.

There is a richness, a variety, a colour and a freedom in God's work of creation which finds reflection in his work of redemption. It is not accidental that Peter prefaces his list of 'gifts of the Spirit' by reference to God's 'varied' grace (1 Pet. 4:10). The word here can be translated, 'many coloured'. Thus the pattern for Christian fellowship is not of a group of people rigidly conforming to some imposed norm and expressing a mirror-image Christian life and experience. Rather it is of a group who are each freely and fully themselves in terms of the gifts and character God has apportioned to each, and yet in whose combined and shared gifts and character the rich and wonderfully attractive grace of God finds expression.

The principle of complementarity can also be applied to the distinction which we drew in chapter three between the local church and other *ad hoc*, peer-group fellowships such as college Christian Unions. In the earlier discussion we noted that the latter were limited in their ability to express the true basis of Christian fellowship which lies in a common participation in Christ. At this point their limitation can be seen as an inherent inability to reflect the full range and richness of God's giving to his people by his Spirit. To use the language of 1 Peter 4:10, God's gracious giving to his people is 'multi-coloured', whereas Christian Unions and their like are by nature monochrome. To put the matter thus is of course exaggerating the uniformity of these groups. God obviously distributes a variety of gifts to his people and that variety is reflected in *any* gathering of Christians. But the full richness and diversity of his giving can be attained and experienced only in contexts where a fuller range of character and experience is reflected than can be attained in any Christian peer group.

(b) For the good of all

The fact that the gifts of the Spirit are given to the people of God 'for the common good', *i.e.* for the contribution they make to the fellowship as a whole, means that an individualistic understanding of the gifts of the Spirit is ruled out. There is therefore no place for exercising our particular gift 'for our own good'. Indeed this is the burden of Paul's discussion on tongue-speaking in 1 Corinthians 14. He contrasts unfavourably the man who speaks in an unknown language to 'edify himself' (verse 4) with the man who 'prophesies' and thereby 'edifies the church'. His great overriding principle as far as this section of 1 Corinthians is concerned is stated in verse 26: 'Let all things be done for edification', *i.e.* for the good of the whole fellowship.

The selfish exercise of a gift of the Spirit can however be done in a more subtle manner. If our gift is of a public nature, such as preaching or teaching, singing or organizing (gifts in other words which bring us public prominence), it is possible to 'use' the public context for our own self-gratification. We can feed our own pride, our self-esteem and our desire for popularity by the manner in which we exercise our ministry among the people of God. Who has not been sickened by the repeated reference of a preacher to his own experiences and achievements, or even those of his family? And who among those who exercise more public gifts dare throw the first stone? God has not given us abilities and gifts primarily for our own good at all. These gifts are given firstly for the Lord's own sake, that he should be glorified and his triumph demonstrated through their being exercised. Secondly, they are for the church's sake, 'for the common good'. We need therefore to be on our guard against 'careerist' tendencies in our thinking and in our attitudes to appointments among God's people. The fellowship is always greater than the individual member. The individual 'minister' exists for the church not the church for the individual. This is no charter for riding rough-shod over individual feelings or convictions. Because God cares for the individual and because attitudes are to be regulated by the principle of *agapē*-love the individual always ought to find a proper respect and understanding. What this truth *does* challenge, however, is all attempts to 'use' the gifts of God as though they were not in fact *gifts* of *God*, *i.e.* ministries, abilities, given by him for his glory and the good of his people.

(c) *Identify your gift*

We obviously need to cultivate the recognition that *all* of God's people have a spiritual gift and ministry, and that we all have a responsibility to exercise it for the common good. We all therefore face the need to identify our gift or gifts. We could make an obvious start with the lists in the New Testament, going through these before the Lord and asking 'Is it this? . . . or this?'

On the basis of the point we noted earlier, however, we would be both unwise and unnecessarily restrictive to confine the gifts of God to those enumerated in the New Testament itself. Even several of these are clearly open-ended, *cf.* 'acts of mercy' (Rom. 12:8), 'service' (Rom. 12:7), 'teachers' (I Cor. 12:28), 'helpers, administrators' (I Cor. 12:28). Küng is prepared to define *charism* (gift of the Spirit) thus: 'Charism signifies the call of God addressed to an individual to a particular ministry in the community which brings with it the ability to fulfil that ministry.'[4]

Thus we want to ask questions such as . . . What opportunities do I have of serving my fellow church members? What can I do towards this or that particular group within the church? Have I gifts of leadership? . . . teaching? . . . preaching? . . . administration? Is there any form of pastoral care which I can exercise? What assets do I have . . . from my upbringing? . . . my leisure? . . . my time? As we seek God's help we will be led to see what our particular gift or gifts may be and obviously they may vary to some extent with our circumstances. Our home with its possibilities for exercising the gift of hospitality (see below, chapter 7) will be less clearly usable in some respects when it is full of growing children than before their arrival, or after they have grown up and gone their own ways. Once we have identified our ministry to the fellowship as a whole then we need to seek actively to dedicate it to the Lord for him to use through us, and then in God's strength to exercise it to his glory and his people's good.

To neglect this process of identifying and exercising our ministry is harmful to the fellowship because it will then lack the irreplaceable contribution which God is calling us to make, however humble and hidden it may be. Our neglecting or hiding of our gift is obviously also displeasing to the Lord himself as two of Jesus' parables make clear (Mt. 25:14–30; Lk. 19:12–27). In both cases to fail to use what the Lord had given received as severe a judgment as active misuse of his gifts.

(d) Each one is important and necessary

In this process we are in effect giving recognition to two complementary truths which the Corinthians had lost sight of in their over-stress on the more spectacular gifts of the Spirit.

(i) Every Christian ministry and every gift of the Spirit is equal in the sight of God (1 Cor. 14:14–25). God does not value the contributions of some more highly than those of others. The determining factor is not the degree of public recognition

nor the popularity or even outward effectiveness of the gift and ministry concerned. What is determinative is the faithful exercise of the gift and ministry which we have received. All ministries and gifts are important and acceptable in his sight, the less prominent equally with the more prominent. Those of us who exercise more prominent forms of ministry need continually to be freed from all illusions of grandeur in this matter. God has no favourite children. The distinction between ordained and unordained, or leaders and led, carries no final significance for him. These distinctions are in the end merely functional and therefore secondary.

That is not to say they are meaningless in every sense. Clearly God wills the good order of his people. The distinction between leader and led is one which the Bible clearly acknowledges. The gifts of the Spirit include the *charismata* of ordained leadership, and a proper recognition of this is part of what is involved in Christian discipleship in any generation, including our own (*cf.* 2 Tim. 1:6-7; 1 Tim. 4:14; 1 Tim. 1:18; Acts 6:1-6; 20:28; Heb. 13:17; 1 Thes. 5:12-13; 1 Cor. 16:18; 1 Pet. 5:1-5; 1 Tim. 5:17; Tit. 1:5-9; 1 Tim. 3:1-13). But these things are not determinative of our intrinsic worth or value to God. In this sense every Christian ministry and every gift of his Spirit is equal in his sight, and ought to be in ours.

(ii) No Christian is self-sufficient—we need each other (1 Cor. 12:19-21). Each member's gift and contribution is required. Not one can be dispensed with. The loss of any member's gift and ministry means the impoverishment of the whole. No one is sufficient in himself and Christian leaders are no exception to this. They need the ministry of those they lead as much as those to whom they minister need them and their ministry of leadership. It is within a caring, praying, sharing fellowship of believing men and women that God intends the Christian life to be lived. Insofar as that is not its context we are accordingly vulnerable. Where such a context is denied us, either because it is not available to us or because in the service of the gospel we have been deliberately led into a situation

where we are pursuing a relatively lonely witness, then we can trust the love and grace of God to make up to us what we lack. But if we lack such a context through our own careless-ness or indifference to the need of it then we need not be surprised if we find the Christian life a struggle and a burden to us. We need each other. It is in the context of the shared life and ministry of a local congregation of God's people that he calls us to serve and live for him.

(e) Do we need to make changes?

In the light of this biblical teaching we cannot avoid taking a look at our church life and asking whether the organization and structures are such as can permit the ministry of the gifts of the Spirit to all the members with the deepening of fellow-ship which it will bring. W. Hahn poses the question thus: 'The question we must ask ourselves is whether such gifts of the Spirit especially among the "laity" may be expressed in the life of our congregations, or whether this is hindered, if not actually excluded, by the too rigid ordering of the church's life and worship.'[5] How we carry this into effect is a matter which requires much loving understanding and sympathy. As we noted above it would be an extraordinary denial of the freedom of the very Spirit who gives his gifts to the people of God if every fellowship were to express this in an identical manner. We must allow for variety and freedom here. There are, however, two normative principles, which are closely related to each other. The first is the centrality of the Word of God. It is in his Word that God's mind and will are disclosed and where all our experiences and patterns and traditions need constantly to be judged and cleansed. Anything which prejudices the cen-trality of the Word cannot claim the support of the Spirit who inspired the Word and is pleased to reaffirm the supreme authority of that Word in the hearts of his people. Secondly, there is the matter of 'building up the church' (1 Cor. 14:12), and therefore the supreme value of the teaching gifts, since nothing is so conducive to spiritual growth as God's truth (1 Pet. 2:2; Jn. 17:17; 2 Tim. 3:16; Acts 6:2-4). This is surely underlined by the fact that a teaching gift or gifts is at the head of each of the five lists of gifts (*cf.* Eph. 4:11–12). John Stott has remarked in this connection:

> 'The apostles' insistence on the priority of teaching has considerable relevance to the contemporary church. All over the world churches are spiritually undernourished owing to the shortage of biblical expositors. In areas where there are mass movements they are crying out for teachers to instruct converts. Because of this dearth of teachers it is sad to see so many people preoccupied with, or even distracted by, gifts of lesser importance.'[6]

When these priorities are recognized and God's gifts truly acknowledged and used among his people one of the most blessed and God-honouring results will be the deepening of their fellowship.

1. *Cf.* T. A. Smail, *Reflected Glory* (Hodder, 1975), ch. 3.
2. H. Küng, *The Church* (Search Press, 1968), p. 186. Also E. Schweizer, *op. cit.*, section 22g. In 1 Cor. 12:31 and 14:1 Paul appears to imply that on occasion further gifts can be sought in prayer, though the granting of them remains with God (1 Cor 12:18).
3. *Cf.* R. P. Martin, *Worship in the Early Church* (Marshall, Morgan and Scott, 1964), pp. 132–133; A. Kuyper, *The Work of the Holy Spirit* (Eerdmans, 1966), pp. 187–189; H. Küng, *op. cit.*, p. 179f.; E. Schweizer, *op. cit.*, p. 203f.; E. M. B. Green, *I Believe in the Holy Spirit* (Hodder, 1975), ch. 10; D. Bridge and D. Phypers, *Spiritual Gifts and the Church* (IVP, 1973), chs. 3 and 4.
4. H. Küng, *op. cit.*, p. 188.
5. W. Hahn, *Worship and Congregation* (Lutterworth, 1963), p. 38.
6. J. R. W. Stott, *Baptism and Fullness*, (IVP, 1975), p. 112.

6

The fellowship meal

We have already noted that the idea of fellowship in the New Testament combines two dimensions. On the one hand our fellowship is grounded in a common participation in the life of the triune God; it is fellowship with God as he has given himself to us in Jesus Christ by the Spirit. On the other hand fellowship also incorporates the dimension of person-to-person relationship; it is fellowship with all those who are participators in the life of God with us. These two dimensions, the vertical relationship with God, and the horizontal relationship with our fellow Christians, are combined in a specific activity of the Christian community which from its very beginnings has been a fundamental expression of Christian fellowship, viz. the fellowship meal, which is variously termed the Lord's Supper, Holy Communion, the eucharist or breaking of bread.

In Acts 2:42 the fundamental elements of the common life of the church from its birth at Pentecost are ennumerated. They comprised the following: 'the apostles' teaching, fellowship, the breaking of bread, and the prayers'. One needs to be careful not to imply too much by 'breaking of bread' here. It probably refers to a simple act of communal fellowship in which the disciples believed the Lord was present among them and in which they recalled his sacrifice on their behalf.

Some interpreters suggest that this reference in the Acts was simply to the continuation of the ordinary meals of fellowship which the disciples had with Jesus during his ministry among them but with no clear reference to his death. Against such a view we need to reaffirm the background to Acts 2:42 as lying in the last supper which Jesus celebrated with the disciples before the cross, where Jesus clearly linked together the Old Testament passover meal, and the new covenant which was to be established through his sacrifice. For the apostles to have established a practice of fellowship meals which denied or neglected this last-supper background would have been unthinkable. Thus we may fairly concur with the verdict of A. J. B. Higgins that as far as the Acts 2:42 reference is concerned 'there can be little doubt that the eucharist is meant';[1] though having said that we are not required to impute to the apostles a fully ordered, liturgically structured service. The importance of the Acts 2 reference, however, is to demonstrate that from the beginning Christian fellowship was linked to the Lord's Supper.

This link between fellowship and the Supper goes back to the two fundamental streams which run into the Christian celebration of the Lord's Supper. Most critics see the last supper as a passover meal reinterpreted by Jesus in terms of his Messianic fulfilment. There is a profound sense of corporate identity here, for Jews celebrating the passover were expressing their oneness with the life and destiny of the chosen people of God. The passover was a community act in which the individual was gathered out of his personal isolation into a profound solidarity with the whole people of God.

The second stream which runs into the Christian celebration, and which in effect represents its basis and foundation, is the last supper itself. At two points during the last supper the corporate aspect was brought clearly to the surface. First, Jesus refers to the new covenant in his blood (1 Cor. 11:25; Mk. 14:24; Mt. 26:28). Now the entire covenant idea in the Old Testament is a profoundly corporate one. The covenant with Abraham gathered into its orbit the future generations of his descendants (Gn. 12:1–3; 17:2–21; Ex. 19:5–6; Dt. 7:6–11; Je. 31:32f.; 11:7f.; etc.); and the reference to the *new* covenant in Jeremiah 31:31ff., which lies behind Jesus' claim, is also clearly addressed to a corporate company. Thus the Lord's Supper as the derivative of the last supper is an ordinance of the new covenant community, an act of the new people of God.

The other explicitly corporate element in the last supper is in Lk. 22:17–18 where Jesus links the celebration of the supper with the coming of the kingdom of God. The coming of the kingdom was established in the death and resurrection of Jesus but awaits his glorious appearing for its full manifestation. This 'two-stage' realization of the promise of the kingdom is perfectly reflected in the Lord's Supper celebration in which we look *back* and rejoice in the action by which the kingdom was established, viz. the sacrifice and triumph of Jesus in his death and resurrection; and *forward* to its full manifestation as we echo the words 'until he comes' (1 Cor. 11:26).

No examination of the biblical notion of fellowship can therefore ignore the Lord's Supper. It is without question a central element in the Christian ideal of fellowship.

In our introductory paragraph we noted that the Lord's Supper focuses the two dimensions of fellowship, the vertical with the Lord and the horizontal with his people. The second of these is our principal concern here. We will begin, however, with at least some examination of the biblical teaching concerning the first.

Fellowship with the Lord

1 Corinthians 10:16–17 is the obvious starting point. Here Paul asserts that to partake of the Supper involves a participation *(koinōnia)* in some sense in the body and blood of Christ *(cf.* 1 Cor. 11:24; Mt. 26:26). The crucial question here of course is the precise nature of this participation. If there is a genuine continuity for Paul between the passover and the Supper then there is a strong implication that in the Christian meal we enter into the cross, the source of our salvation, just as the Jew was enabled through the feast to relive the experience of those who came out from the Egyptian bondage. It is also a fair inference that if Paul regarded sharing in the idolatrous feasts of pagan friends as running the danger of

Christians becoming 'partners with demons', then partaking of the Christian meal also involves a real sharing with Christ himself. It is difficult to see how Paul could have used such an argument unless he had a basic conviction that participation in any such rite implied a real encounter with the spiritual reality in whose name it was conducted. Thus for the Christian to share in the Lord's Supper involves a sharing in the Lord whose redemption is signified in the elements of bread and wine.

The Lord's Supper, then, is more than a simple act of remembrance, a sort of Christian Poppy Day, in which we recall the giving of life on our behalf and the cost of our freedom. It *is* that, of course, as the Lord himself states: 'Do this in remembrance of me' (1 Cor. 11:24). But it is more than that. It is also a point of fellowship with the risen and exalted Lord. This does not necessitate any sacramentalist notion of the automatic 'presence' of the Lord in the elements themselves for Jesus is met and experienced in the Supper on no other basis than that upon which he is met and experienced in any other context, viz. *by faith alone*. As Calvin put it, 'Men bear away from this sacrament no more than they gather with the vessel of faith.'[2] A living faith in Christ as Lord and Saviour is the only ground upon which we can derive any blessing or fellowship with him in the meal. But approaching the Supper on that basis, there we see portrayed in vivid symbol the costly act of sacrifice by which our sin was atoned for, and there we meet again our blessed Lord, and taste again in faith the benefits of his passion. There we feed on him by faith in the Spirit and are gathered into communion with him in his ascended glory.

Fellowship with one another

When we turn our attention to the Lord's Supper as *fellowship with one another* we find Paul saying, 'We who are many are one body, for we all partake of the one bread' (1 Cor. 10:17). While this verse is not easy to interpret, the stress on the unity of those who share the meal together is clear.[3] The single loaf which was broken and shared by all spoke clearly of the single life which all partakers shared in the one Lord.

In the following chapter (11:17–31) Paul deals with certain abuses of the Supper. In Corinth it appears to have been the custom for some at least to share a meal together in the normal social sense before coming to the actual communion service and Lord's Supper. Paul sees the unworthy behaviour evidenced there (18 and 21) as 'despising the church of God' (22) and rebukes them sharply. With such goings on as preliminary there can be no genuine celebration of the Lord's Supper, indeed in such a context, 'It is not the Lord's Supper that you eat' (verse 20).

For the apostle Paul there could be no real participation in the Lord's Supper where there was no real unity of spirit and behaviour among the participants. The Lord's Supper is profaned where it does not flow out of real unity among those who share it. Unless there was real fellowship in the social meal before the Lord's Supper there could be no genuine celebration of the Supper which followed. Thus the importance of the horizontal dimension is brought clearly to the surface. One New Testament scholar makes the application of this passage in this way: 'A congregation which does not eat hotdogs in real fellowship is not able to celebrate the Lord's Supper in the right way.'[4] In our cultural context we might perhaps wish to substitute drinking a cup of tea or coffee for the eating of hot-dogs, but the point is surely well taken. The relationships between participants is crucial to the proper celebration of the eucharist.

It is going beyond the biblical evidence to argue as some do that the celebration of the Supper actually creates unity. The fellowship in the Lord by the Spirit must be there already as a necessary presupposition. But there is surely enough in the passages in 1 Corinthians and elsewhere (Acts 2:42) to permit us to conclude that the unity and fellowship which we experience in Christ through the Holy Spirit will find an important, divinely ordained expression in the celebration of the Lord's Supper; and hence that the Supper is a significant means for the strengthening of Christian fellowship.

If this is so then our general failure to take the horizontal aspects of the Lord's Supper as seriously as the vertical ones is a serious one. Andrew Murray puts the issue clearly: 'How often have the guests at Jesus' table sat next to one another for years in succession without knowing or loving one another, or helping one another. Many a one has sought after closer communion with the Lord and not found it, because he would have the Head alone without the body . . . would that it were thoroughly understood—Jesus must be loved, and honoured, and served, and known in His members.'[5] This last sentence is of very wide reference indeed and serves to underline the concern of this whole book. You cannot have the head without the body. The Christ who comes to us is a Christ who comes clothed with his body. We cannot therefore expect to grow in relationship with him if we are all the while careless of our relationships with his people. We cannot accept the head and reject the body. Our relationships with the members of our local fellowship will be a factor of real significance for our spiritual growth. In the Lord's Supper these two dimensions are drawn explicitly together.

It is worthwhile exploring one or two applications of this truth to the way we celebrate the Lord's Supper.

First, the evidence we have examined from Scripture underlines the importance of the Supper. True fellowship will naturally find expression in the communion of the Lord's table. This is another of the points at which the distinction between a church and a more *ad hoc* kind of Christian group such as a Christian Union or works Christian fellowship becomes apparent. These groups are unquestionably of great significance for living the Christian life in the particular context of a college or factory. Indeed they are virtually essential for an effective witness to Christ to be borne in such places. But they are not churches. They are 'peer group' organizations which unite a narrow segment of society on the basis of common, temporary concerns. They lack the richness, variety and permanence of a local Christian congregation. They also are not constituted as a church with all the fullness of congregational life including regular celebration of the sacraments.

There are occasional contexts in which the celebration of the Supper by such a group is appropriate, *e.g.* conferences, house parties, *etc.* But that is not the norm, nor can it be where a group lacks many of the essentials of full congregational life.

Secondly, we need to take the horizontal dimension of the Supper very seriously. One of the results of our loss of this aspect has been the development of an approach to the Supper which is highly individualistic. People even talk sometimes of 'making my communion', and the whole thing becomes an individualistic, pious act undertaken by the individual in expression of their personal devotion to the Lord.[6] Without wishing to minimize what such practice means to those who engage in it we can surely point out on the basis of the New Testament that such an understanding falls far short of Scripture, and is even a serious misunderstanding. The Lord's Supper is an act of the *whole* church. It is an act of the congregation, and it is in such a context that it needs consciously to be celebrated. We need to avoid allowing sentimental associations to determine our biblical and theological interpretation. Obviously circumstances do arise, *e.g.* illness or other forms of individual confinement, where the Supper can be celebrated only in an individual setting. Even then however the celebrant of the Supper can frequently make arrangements for one or two church members to accompany him as representative of the whole congregation. Certainly where there is no such restriction the Supper needs to be brought clearly into the congregational setting.

The loss of the corporate, however, can also take place in a subtler manner even where the form of the Supper is congregational. It is common for participants in the Supper to spend much if not all of the time during the communion service with eyes closed in meditation and prayer. Again one would hesitate to be legalistic or to be unworthily critical of what is clearly a real means of grace, nor would one wish to suggest that an attitude of prayer is other than a wholly proper attitude in which to share the meal. However, if we are to take the 'fellowship' aspects seriously must we not at some point deliberately open our eyes and look upon the people of the Lord, our brethren who meet around the table with us, and who with us constitute the body of Christ? In other words may we not need to make some provision for the corporateness of the Supper in the way in which we order it, since by our very zeal and piety we can in fact return to that individualistic understanding and practice which we have already seen reason to question?

Thirdly, Scripture in 1 Corinthians 11:28 encourages self-examination *before* participating. From what we have seen concerning the horizontal dimension of our fellowship in the Supper, ought not a main area for self-examination be our relationships with those who sit around us in the congregation? Matthew 5:23f., with its stress upon leaving an offering at the alter and first being reconciled with our brother may have some pertinence here. It would be a bold step to allow time before a service for members to put matters right between them and, of course, could lead to artificiality and embarrassment of an unhelpful kind. However, it would certainly be to the point to encourage this kind of self-examination before the celebration of the meal together (*cf.* Mk. 11:25; Mt. 6:11–18; Eph. 4:32; Col. 3:13).

Fourthly, if the horizontal fellowship aspect is so important we surely need to make provision in the symbolism and action of the Supper for its expression. The common habit of dicing the bread for example needs to be questioned. The New Testament practice was pretty clearly that of using a single loaf (1 Cor. 10:17) and through our hygienic scruples we in fact effectively destroy much of the basic biblical symbolism and help perpetuate the unbiblical, individualistic understanding of the Supper which we noted above. A common cup was also very likely to have been the New Testament practice as at the last supper (1 Cor. 11:25; Mk. 14:23). One properly hesitates to be over-legalistic here. Liberty must be permitted and those who have scruples must be respected (*cf.* Rom. 14). However, we equally ought not to be insensitive to the power of symbolism, particularly where it would have the appearance of biblical precedent, and it would appear right to try and let the symbolism of the Supper as far as possible reflect the spiritual realities which underly it.

Other forms of expressing fellowship at the Supper such as hand-shakes, verbal greetings, *etc.*, *can* become unnatural and even embarassing if imposed too rigidly. There is need for sensitivity and care. It is surely to miss the whole point if we cause breaches of relationship and make people feel 'out of it' through some activity which is precisely intended to express our unity and oneness. However, in whatever form it is done, *something* surely needs to be attempted, at very least the sharing in a hymn or song of praise, for the horizontal cannot be excluded without the meaning of the Supper being seriously affected and the wholeness of the meal lost for us.

Here then is a very important way in which true fellowship will express itself and be deepened, the joyous and yet awesome celebration of the Supper of the Lord.

1. A. J. B. Higgins, *The Lord's Supper in the New Testament* (SCM, 1952), p. 56.
2. Calvin, *Institutes*, IV, 17. 33.
3. A. Robertson and A. Plummer, *I Corinthians* (*International Critical Commentary*, T. and T. Clark, 1914), p. 214f.; L. Morris, *The First Epistle of Paul to the Corinthians* (IVP, 1958), p. 146.
4. E. Schweizer, art. in *Interpretation*, XIII, 1959, p. 401.
5. A. Murray, *The Lord's Table* (Moody Press, 1962), p. 84.
6. *Cf.* A. R. George, *op. cit.*, p. 174.

7

The practice of fellowship

At the end of chapter four we noted the need for our love to express itself in practice. 'Love must not be a matter of words or talk; it must be genuine, and show itself in action' (1 Jn. 3:18, NEB). In this chapter we will explore some of the ways in which love 'showed itself in action' in the New Testament churches.

Burden-bearing

One of the commonest titles for a Christian priest or minister is 'pastor'. It is a title with strong biblical roots (Pss. 78:70–72; 23:1–4; Is. 40:11; Je. 3:15; 10:21; Ezk. 34:1–31). The ordained Christian minister, or his equivalent, is called to be an under-shepherd to the Chief Shepherd and to 'tend the flock of God' (1 Pet. 5:2). The danger of this picture however is that it can carry the implication that all the caring for the flock is the responsibility of the minister or leader. It can obscure the complementary New Testament truth that the sheep also have a responsibility to care for each other. Pastoral ministry is never simply the ministry of the pastor. Pastoral ministry must be a shared ministry of the whole congregation. As 1 Corinthians 12:24f. reminds us, one of the primary reasons for God gathering his people into local groups in churches and distributing the rich variety of his gifts amongst them is that 'the members may have the same care for one another'[1] (cf. verse 25; Eph. 4:32; Phil. 2:4).

'Bear one another's burdens', Paul exhorts the Galatians

(Gal. 6:2), and he says something similar to the Thessalonians, 'Help the weak' (1 Thes. 5:14), and to the Romans, 'We who are strong ought to bear with the failings of the weak' (Rom. 15:1). It is crucially important in applying these injunctions that we do not classify 'strong' and 'weak' too rigidly. No doubt there are more mature members of every Christian fellowship who would normally fulfil the role of the 'strong', and equally there are the comparatively immature members who would normally fulfil the role of the 'weak'. But these are never once-for-all classifications. There are times when we are all 'weak' and in the need of the support of our fellow members. The Christian psychiatrist Paul Tournier in a section of one of his books, entitled 'The need for support', makes just this point. Meeting his pastor one day he remarked, 'You never visit me.' 'Oh, you don't need it,' came the retort, 'I go and see the lost sheep', to which Tournier poignantly comments, 'Am I not also a lost sheep? . . . I have seen committed Christians weeping in my counselling room, "pillars of the church" . . . on whom everyone depended, but whom no one troubled to help in their personal difficulties.'[2] The plain truth is that we are all weak much of the time, in spite of the often frantic efforts we make to hide the fact from one another and from ourselves. We all stand in constant need of a burden-bearing fellowship.

Lest this be thought to be a rather low view of the Christian life it is worth noting that in this confession of weakness we are in the best of company. Paul's letters have several confessions of real weakness. He reminds the Corinthians that his public ministry among them had been 'in weakness and in much fear and trembling' (1 Cor. 2:3; cf. 4:10). At a later point he and his colleagues were 'so utterly, unbearably crushed that we despaired of life itself' (2 Cor. 1:8). He is 'afflicted . . ., perplexed . . ., persecuted . . ., struck down' (4:8–9). And in his famous autobiographical passage in 2 Corinthians 12 he refers to his 'thorn (lit. stake) in the flesh' and talks freely of his 'weakness' (cf. verses 5–9; 13:4). Indeed these very weaknesses are cause not for shame but for boasting (12:9), for he has come to see that they are the secret of Christ's power in his life. Not surprisingly therefore we find Paul speaking of his need of the 'shoring-up' of his fellow Christians (Rom. 1:12; 2 Cor. 7:6).

There is a sense in which we may even include the Lord Jesus Christ in this company of the 'weak'. The obvious point of reference here is to his death on the cross where he was 'crucified in weakness' in order to become the means of our salvation and atonement. There can be no profounder demonstration of utter weakness than Jesus upon the cross. He is there a picture of utter helplessness, stripped of all his human dignity, forsaken by his friends and followers, the object of the insults and jeers of the mob and the religious authorities and leaders of his people.

Two of his words from the cross bring this starkly home to us: 'I thirst', he cried. The one through whom the very oceans were formed cries out in the agony of dehydration for the relief of a few drops of water, and is thus in his weakness dependent upon the whim of his own creatures. 'My God, my God, why hast thou forsaken me?' he cried, as in the mystery of redeeming love God the Son carried his identification with sinners even to the terrible limit of bearing the wrath of God against us. In that moment Jesus experienced a helplessness which has had no equal in all the long story of man.

However, may we not see this principle operating through his ministry? The question may at least be raised in connection with the ministry of the twelve disciples. The call of the twelve had a variety of purposes. The number twelve is surely a deliberate echo of the number of the tribes of Israel, and gives expression to Jesus' consciousness that through his mission he was to inaugurate the new covenant between man and God and reconstitute the covenant community as the people of the Messiah, the new Israel. The selection of the twelve obviously also had strategic purposes in terms of his training of them for their future responsibilities. As the leaders of the new community of the kingdom of God they were called to be 'with him' and hence to be equipped to be 'sent out' by him (Mk. 3:14; Lk. 22:28).

Granting that these were the primary purposes of their

calling, can we not also think of a purpose in terms of their ministry *to* Jesus? The exegetical basis here is not a strong one so one cannot make more than a suggestion, but if he was 'made like his brethren in every respect' and 'able to sympathize with our weaknesses' (Heb. 2:17; 4:15) does this not permit us to think of him at times finding strength in others? The nearest to a clear statement of this is in the garden of Gethsemane where Jesus' plea, 'My soul is very sorrowful, even unto death . . . watch with me', seems to indicate his longing in that moment for a sense of human comradeship, a need for fellowship in the agony of his temptation. It is perhaps pertinent to observe from the Gospel records the two occasions when Jesus is given angelic ministration. The first was in the wilderness after the assaults of the tempter (Mt. 4:11), the second was in the garden of Gethsemane as he wrestled with the awful prospect of the cross and all it would mean (Lk. 22:43). On both occasions the disciples were not at hand, in the former case because they had not yet been called, in the latter because they were asleep. Were the disciples themselves God's ministering angels the rest of the time? We cannot say for certain, but there is one other saying which might lend support to such a view, Luke 22:28, where Jesus describes the twelve as those who have 'continued with me in my trials'.

Thus the recognition that we have 'weaknesses' is not something concerning which we need necessarily feel any sense of guilt. We are in good company. It is surely relevant to this truth that the vast bulk of the Bible's direct teaching concerning the Christian life occurs in letters addressed to churches, *i.e.* to corporate groups of Christians. It is in *that* context, in the setting of a burden-bearing fellowship, that God intends the Christian life to be lived.

It is in this light that we perhaps need to put a question mark against some holiness teaching which sets forth the Christian ideal in terms of what one might describe as 'the omnicompetent individual'. By this view the man or woman we are all to strive to become is an individual of all-round spiritual competence, who is able to cope with any pressure, to meet every obstacle, to deal with every situation, and to experience a life of unbroken victory over sin and Satan. One wonders whether this 'image' of the Christian life does not owe much more to Christian biographers than to the Bible. One recognizes immediately that this ideal has unquestionably produced in the past some remarkable examples of Christian character; but it has equally driven many others to a lonely struggle ending in despair and disillusionment, or to what is possibly worse, the hypocrisy of a double-standard life, whereby we struggle to maintain the omnicompetent image in public and know ourselves to be something very different behind the scenes. The biblical ideal by contrast appears much more that of the omnicompetent Christian fellowship, where in the total life of the whole body the weaknesses and limitations of each are taken account of and complemented by the strengths of the whole.

A great danger of this kind of emphasis of course is that it may seem to lower the standards of personal holiness set out in Scripture and hence to represent an easier, lower path for discipleship. If this were so then all that we have said above stands immediately self-condemned. The biblical summons to holy living can never be muted or compromised without dishonour being done to God, who as the Holy One calls us to honour him in conforming to his image and likeness. There can be no muting of the call to live lives which are imbued with the spirit of repentance from sin and the constant prayer to be made more like the Lord Jesus Christ in every area of our experience.

Such a demand, and such a life-style, however, do not rule out the equally clear insistence of the Scriptures on the corporate setting of this life of holiness. Putting this same truth in another way—we need to recognize that the Christ to whose image we are to be conformed is the Christ of his body, the church, and that we will produce the image of Christ in the context of the whole body's life and mutual ministries (Eph. 4:13–16). Holiness void of love is simply not biblical holiness. And if all this is true then we need to face up to our real responsibility not just for our own Christian life and growth but also for the Christian life and growth of all the others in our local church and fellowship. We are to 'bear one another's burdens'.

Part of the difficulty in carrying this into effect, of course, lies in the sad fact that our local church is, in many cases, just about the last place in the world we would dare to bring our sense of weakness. James Philip in his great book, *Christian Maturity*, puts a searching question to us: 'Am I the kind of Christian that a man who had failed would instinctively shrink from and say 'Oh no, I could never confide in *him*', or would he feel free to come to me in trouble?'[3] This is far from being an idle question, because people who had failed felt drawn to Jesus like a magnet (Mt. 11:19; Lk. 5:29f.; 7:37ff.; 19:1ff.; Jn. 4:7ff.). If we are not the kind of folks that people find it easy to confide in then it may be high time we asked why. It is possible to be energetically 'holy' and yet fearfully un-Christlike. If the Christian who has failed does not detect in us something of the compassion and sympathy of Christ (which is of course not the same as a weak toleration of sin and evil, witness Jesus) then something has gone terribly wrong with our sanctification. Likewise, if our church fellowship is not the kind of company where the man who has failed feels welcome and loved, the kind of place where he can face up to life again and begin to work his way back to the standards and patterns from which he has stumbled, then our church is denying the very spirit of its Lord no matter how orthodox its testimony. The Canadian writer Bruce Larson is making the same point in a vivid way when he writes:

'The neighbourhood bar is possibly the best counterfeit there is for the fellowship Christ wants to give his Church. It's an imitation dispensing liquor instead of grace, escape rather than reality, but it is a permissive, accepting and inclusive fellowship. It is unshockable. It is democratic. You can tell people secrets and they usually don't tell others or even don't want to. The bar flourishes not because most people are alcoholics, but because God has put into the human heart the desire to know and be known, to love and be loved, and so many seek a counterfeit at the price of a few beers.'[4]

One of the blocks in the way of achieving the kind of closeness of relationship which a 'burden-bearing fellowship' expresses is that many of our Christian churches and fellowships are too large for this kind of thing to be practically possible. It may be that a first step towards realizing this ideal would be to look seriously at our church structures to see whether there cannot be found room for the smaller, more informal kind of contact where fellowship of this depth and reality can be fostered. The New Testament churches were on the whole quite small groups consisting probably of no more than a few dozen members (cf. Rom. 16:3ff.; Phm. 1f.). History would seem to support this kind of courageous restructuring. The Methodist Class meeting, the Praying Societies in Scottish church life, the fellowship meeting in the East African revival, and the experience of contemporary Christian groups like All Souls' Church in the centre of London,[5] and the laymen's groups in Texas sponsored by Keith Miller,[6] all underline the possibilities here.

Prayer

One of the first expressions of the new life at Pentecost was a fellowship which gave prominence to 'the breaking of the bread and the prayers' (Acts 2:42). We have already referred to the first of these. The reference to *the* prayers is tantalizing. Did it mean the formal prayers in the temple? Acts 3:1f. indicates that the apostles, and in all probability the rest of the church, attended the temple services, particularly the times of prayer (Acts 3:1). 'The prayers' almost certainly would include these formal prayers. We have already noted, however, that the 'breaking of bread' does not belong to the setting of the temple liturgy but, as in Acts 2:46, is set 'in their homes'. It would be surprising therefore if prayer did not also spill over into the home context, and there are two other references in Acts to support this supposition. In 4:23ff., the return of the apostles from prison and trial is the signal for a spontaneous corporate prayer meeting (verses 24-33) which was given a remarkable token of having been heard by the Lord (verse 31). In chapter 12, Peter's imprisonment and impending execution is the cause of prayer by the church in a home in Jerusalem (12:12). Hence we can confirm the impression derived from Acts 2 that the early church was a community imbued with a spirit of prayer. If *our* concern for one another is genuine it will inevitably express itself in prayer for one another.

The instances noted in Acts are of corporate gatherings. The injunction of James 5:16, 'Pray for one another' (with verse 14, the prayer of the elders over a sick member, in the background), is also probably corporate in its immediate reference. Although we commonly stress the importance of corporate prayer in terms of its relationship to the preaching of the gospel and the success of the church's various activities, and rightly so, we ought not to miss the contribution which it represents towards the deepening of fellowship among the members. Few things are more conducive to a deepened commitment to one another than the experience of sharing together in earnest and Spirit-inspired prayer. Nor should we allow the fact that only a minority of the church or group attend the prayer meetings to cause us to be deflected from this crucial ministry. Obviously the more folks that can be drawn into the praying fellowship the better, and we should not be insensitive to the difficulties which some Christian folks have in sharing in prayer in this way. Things like over-long and over-generalized prayers by 'elder brethren' may need a gentle but firm handling. The importance of a lively and earnest prayer fellowship to the life and effectiveness of any church is such as to override the feelings of any one individual, even if he be the minister! Here is an important means of expressing our love for one another and deepening the fellowship—praying together.

But prayer also has a profound personal dimension. If we love the people of God we will surely find time to speak to God about them, and seek his blessing upon them. Jesus again is our great exemplar. In the shadow of his great testing, he tells Peter 'I have prayed for you' (Lk. 22:32), and assures him of restoration and a renewal of his ministry after his denial. It is surely right to see Jesus' extended intercessions and prayers as being directed to a significant degree towards the disciples (*cf.* Lk. 6:12f.; 9:18, 28; 11:1; Mt. 14:23ff.). Further, Jesus' ministry of intercession for his own cannot be confined to the period of his earthly life but carries over into his present high-priestly work for us (Heb. 7:25; *cf.* 2:17f.; 4:15f.). It is unnecessary and even mistaken to picture the exalted Jesus in a constant posture of prayer (*cf.* Acts 7:55; Rev. 5:6f.) but the truth that Christ bears our needs into the presence of God and constantly sustains us in his grace is a truth to be laid hold of with joy. In Romans 8:26-27 Paul also speaks of an intercessory ministry of the Holy Spirit. Thus to engage in prayer for one another is to emulate the Godhead. There can be no higher incentive for it, and no stronger argument in its support.

The apostle Paul is another great biblical example of intercessory prayer and he makes a number of references to the duty of engaging in it (Eph. 6:18; 1:16; Rom. 12:12; Col. 1:9; 4:2; 1 Thes. 5:17; 1:2; 1 Tim. 2:1). It is worth remarking upon the content of the apostle's prayers for his fellow Christians. His prayers concentrate on their spiritual growth (Eph. 1:17-19; 3:14-20; Phil. 1:9-11; Col. 1:9-12; 1 Thes. 3:12-13). It is remarkable how frequently we depart from this pattern by concentrating in our prayers for fellow Christians upon their bodily needs, and insofar as we pray for spiritual needs at all we pray for the spiritual conversion of non-Christians. One is sometimes tempted to think that the only sure way to get Christians to pray for one is to fall under a bus and be carted off to hospital! Thus our habit of praying for the souls of non-Christians and the bodies of Christians is out of step with biblical patterns. In fact the New Testament knows surprisingly little of specific prayers for the conversion of specific non-Christians. This is not to suggest of course that such prayer was not offered or that it is anything other than a proper matter for our prayers today. Nor equally is it to suggest any impropriety in praying for very practical needs as far as our fellow Christians are concerned. But it *is* to highlight the need for regular prayer *also* for one another's spiritual growth. It might be a salutary exercise to use one of Paul's prayers above as a basis on the next occasion we engage in prayer for our fellow church members.

The practice of some churches and fellowships of dividing the membership up into groups in a daily prayer list is helpful in this connection. Provided we do not fall into a legalistic pattern, and provided we do not simply rattle through a list of names with never a thought for the people themselves and their circumstances, it can be a real promotion of fellowship as well, of course, as being a channel of grace as God hears and answers our prayers. If we take the time to focus imaginatively upon each person and surround them deliberately and earnestly with our love and concern as we pray for them then the contribution of such praying to our fellowship with them, and hence to the quality of fellowship throughout the whole church, will be a very significant one.

Where there is care for each other there will be prayer for each other; and where there is real prayer for each other there will be a deeper care for each other. 'Pray for one another.'

Confession

James 5:16 urges us, 'Confess your sins to one another.' Obviously the primary direction in which our prayers of confession are to be directed is to the Lord. Confession of sin is a continuous feature of the Christian's relationship with the Lord. Although all our sin is forgiven and all its guilt removed through the once-for-all sacrifice of Christ at Calvary the Christian needs to come again and again to the Lord confessing specific sins and seeking forgiveness and renewal of relationship with him (*cf.* 1 Jn. 1:8–10).

The reference in James, however, reminds us that there is a place in the Christian life for confession to fellow Christians. It is certainly to be doubted whether this reference is sufficient to justify the practice of aural confession to a priest as an intrinsic part of the church's ministry. Our confessions are first to the Lord and we do not require to be assured of his pardon by any intermediary. However, when the sins in question have been committed against a fellow Christian, and are of such a nature that he is aware of the sin and it constitutes a breach of fellowship between us, then there *is* need to put this exhortation in James chapter 5 into practice.

Jesus speaks of something akin to this in the Sermon on the Mount, where he teaches that we cannot worthily bring an offering to God if our lives are out of harmony with our brethren. Hence the need to 'leave your gift . . . and go; first be reconciled to your brother, and then come and offer your gift' (Mt. 5:24). This is in keeping with the way in which the Bible holds together the dimensions of our relationship with God and our relationship with men, as we saw in the second chapter. It is impossible to separate these into water-tight compartments. Thus an unreconciled relationship with a fellow Christian will affect the reality of our relationship with God.

'I'm sorry' and 'I apologize' are easily written but can sometimes be among the hardest words in the language to pronounce. Yet how many churches are divided and devoid of God's blessing for lack of these words being spoken. The real barrier is our pride which is deeply hurt by our failure and which doesn't even want to admit to responsibility at all. It is very humbling to have to go to another Christian and ask for forgiveness. In that moment we are stripped of all our pretensions and of all the things which we use to inflate our image and attainments before others. In that moment we are reduced to our real size, to what we really are: poor and needy sinners living by grace alone. But then, of course, that is quite simply the truth about us, just as it is the truth about the person to whom we are making our confession and whose forgiveness we are seeking. They too have their failures, they too need God's mercy every day of their lives. When we say 'I'm sorry' we are being real before our Christian brother or sister, and in that moment of confession, as we present ourselves to them in our vulnerability and weakness we invite them to become real too. We give them the opportunity to step out from behind *their* curtains of sham and pretence and to stand with us in the presence of the Lord waiting for his grace. Often it is an invitation which they find it impossible to resist, and so they in turn are able to see themselves as they truly are, and to accept it because in the act of confession we are accepting what *we* really are. The fear of being known for what we truly are is removed and we can discover a whole new dimension of relationship.

The history of revival contains many testimonies to the working out of this principle. As one Christian has been prepared to confess his wrongs and to stand as he really is, 'in the light' before God, so others have been rebuked for their failures, and so in turn others have been challenged, and thus God's Spirit has been able to move into the fellowship and through them into the wider community. This was precisely the pattern in the East African revival, but it has been so on many other occasions. What might God not do in our church or fellowship if we were able really to put things 'in the light' with our fellow Christians?

Perhaps a word of caution is in order however. It would appear that this 'confession' relates to matters which are points of conscious contention between Christians. We need to avoid extending this too widely, either by artificially creating matters for confession or by inflating trivial issues out of all proportion. We also need to be sensitive to the dangers of confessing too freely matters which can prompt unhealthy thoughts and imagination. We ought not to get this element out of perspective. Confession of sin where there is a real matter of contention between two Christians is a biblically recognized practice. But it is not given the central place in the New Testament's account of Christian living and we need to avoid getting it out of proportion as far as the life of fellowship is concerned.

Where causes of friction *have* arisen, however, the fellowship of the church can really grow only when matters are put right. We owe it to the Lord, whose body the church is, and we owe it to our brother or sister whom we have wronged, to be ready to swallow our pride, face reality, go to them and say, simply and sincerely, 'I'm sorry . . .' Fellowship of the kind and quality we are discussing in this book lies, for many a church, on the further side of these two words.

Exhortation

As far as the fourth expression of active caring is concerned Hebrews 3:13 will serve as our key text, 'Exhort one another every day . . . that none of you may be hardened by the deceitfulness of sin.' The word for 'exhort', *parakaleō*, can carry several meanings and is rendered variously in the RSV by 'comfort' (*e.g.* 2 Cor. 7:6); 'exhort' (*e.g.* Acts. 2:40; 16:40; Rom. 12:8); 'beseech' (*e.g.* Mt. 8:5; 2 Cor. 12:8) and 'console' (*e.g.* Lk. 6:24; 2:25). (*Cf.* also Rom. 1:12; 15:2; Eph. 4:16; Col. 3:16; 1 Thes. 5:11; Heb. 10:24f.; Jude 20.) As far as relations with our fellow member are concerned these scriptures teach the need to be ready to exhort and encourage him, to 'strengthen his hand in God' (1 Sa. 23:16). We do not find this easy of course. Our traditional reserve inhibits us, and we may feel a proper hesitation in referring to spiritual issues lest we cause embarrassment or appear to be standing in judgment. However, to fail to engage in this ministry at any level could be an expression of a lack of real care. Barnabas is the great New Testament example here. His name literally means 'son of *paraklēsis*' (Acts 4:36). When one recalls that Christ uses exactly this term for the Holy Spirit, the Paraclete (John 14:6; 14:26; 15:26; 16:7), and that Barnabas is elsewhere described as a man 'full of the Holy Spirit' (Acts 11:24) one has the necessary terms for an equation of the encouraging, strengthening ministry of the Holy Spirit with the encouraging, strengthening ministry which each believer is to exercise towards his brethren.

Hospitality

We come now to a highly practical way of deepening and expressing Christian fellowship. To love means to be willing to share, and sharing includes sharing our homes. The practice of hospitality is on the whole taken for granted in Scripture rather than explicitly commanded. That such conduct was appropriate to God's people is implied in a number of Old Testament passages (Gn. 18:1ff.; Ex. 2:20; Dt. 23:4; Jdg. 13:15; 19:15; 1 Ki. 17:10ff.; 2 Ki. 4:8ff.). Our Lord, as one who had 'nowhere to lay his head' (Mt. 8:20), was obviously deeply dependent upon the hospitality of others (Mt. 8:14; 26:6; Lk. 5:29; 7:36f.; 19:5), and in particular the home of Mary, Martha and Lazarus at Bethany (Jn. 11:1f.; Lk. 10:38f.).

When he sent out the twelve, and the seventy, Jesus expected them to be given hospitality (Mt. 10:9f.; Lk. 10:4f.), and he regarded the refusal of such as tantamount to a rejection of their message (Mt. 10:14; Lk. 10:10f.). The parable of Matthew 25:31–46 includes a clear reference to hospitality—'I was a stranger and you welcomed me' (Mt. 25:35). In the terms of this parable the giving or withholding of hospitality when we are in a position to offer it is a decisive indication of the presence or absence of real spiritual life.

The New Testament letters have some quite direct teaching on the subject. Romans 12:13 summons us to 'practise hospitality' (cf. Gal. 6:10; Col. 4:10; Phm. 22). 1 Timothy 3:2 and Titus 1:8 put the practice of hospitality high on the list of a minister's qualifications; this should be a notable feature of any Christian minister: the openness of his home to his people and to all those in need. The fullest statement is probably that in 1 Peter 4:9; 'Practise hospitality ungrudgingly to one another', and this reference occurs interestingly enough in the context of teaching on the gifts of the Spirit (cf. verse 10). Thus we cannot complain of not having been given a gift of the Holy Spirit if God has given us a home into which we can welcome people. A home is a gift of God which he wants us to invest in the interests of the kingdom of God. Finally, Hebrews 13:2 urges us to 'show hospitality to strangers' as an expression of 'brotherly love'. This is an indication that hospitality is not simply to be offered to those whom we know well; it should be extended also to the 'stranger' among the people of God in token of our welcoming them into our Christian fellowship.

It is difficult to avoid the implications of such clear, practical teaching. If we love our Christian brethren as we ought to, and if we really mean business in this matter of deepening the fellowship between us, then we will invite them into our homes. If we fail to obey this clear biblical teaching, or if we carry it out in an unbiblical manner (*i.e.* 'grudgingly'; *cf.* 1 Pet. 4:9), then we really have no grounds for complaint about the lack of fellowship in our church or Christian group.

What deepening of fellowship would result if we were all to start using our homes in this way. We could make a start next weekend, and where better than with someone who is not normally in the limelight or high on the popularity list in the congregation? The author recalls a church where on certain Sundays half the congregation prepared double Sunday lunches and the other half were their guests. And just to make it really impartial the names of the guests were drawn out of a hat! To some this may seem a little artificial. Yet it will not surprise the reader to know that the church concerned was, and remains, renowned for the quality of its fellowship.

In the end our homes are not 'ours'. Like everything else we have they belong ultimately to the Lord. We are stewards of our homes for him. How many Christians could testify, like the author of this book, to how great a contribution has been made to their Christian growth and progress particularly in times of discouragement or loneliness by the 'sacrament' of a Christian home opened and shared in Christ's name. Nor is this ministry to be confined too rigidly to hospitality extended to fellow Christians. In a day when fewer and fewer non-Christians are likely to cross the threshold of a church or respond to invitations to 'come and worship with us' in a church building, so very many will still respond gratefully to an invitation to share the hospitality of our homes.[7]

Quite apart from evangelistic considerations, or even the thought of what our offer of hospitality might do towards the encouragement of our fellow Christians, there remain the words of our Lord, 'Inasmuch as you did it unto one of the least of these my brethren, you did it unto me.' We can surely find the time and make the effort to entertain *him*!

Finance

The New Testament has some very pertinent things to say to us all about the financial side of fellowship. We begin with three of our Lord's parables. Firstly, there is the parable of the sheep and goats (Mt. 25:31-46). If we follow the interpretation indicated in an earlier chapter then the evidence of our being God's regenerate children—on the strength of which evidence our eternal destiny can be decided—is our *practical* love of the 'brethren' (Mt. 25:40). Money is not directly mentioned, of course, but is certainly involved in this parable by implication. Secondly, there is the parable of the unjust steward (Lk. 16:1-13). Jesus does not condone the astute trickery of the steward, but he does point out the general lesson that we are to use our 'unrighteous mammon' (Lk. 16:9) for eternal spiritual profit, and the particular case he mentions is its use to 'make friends', *i.e.* to establish and deepen relationships which will mean the growth and building up of God's kingdom. Thirdly, there is the parable of the pounds (Lk. 19:12-27). Whatever else the 'pounds' may be referring to they certainly must be applied to the literal pounds which each month and year pass through our hands. We are to spend this as in the sight of God and in such a way as to bring profit for our King. In this last instance the use of money for our spiritual brethren is not as explicit as in the other two parables, but it is one of the obvious areas for the financial investment which our Lord expects of us (verses 16f.).

The command of Romans 12:13 is quite unambiguous: 'Contribute to the needs of the saints.' Timothy is urged by Paul to teach wealthy church members 'to be . . . liberal and generous' (1 Tim. 6:18). Hebrews 13:16 exhorts us: 'Share what you have, for such sacrifices are pleasing to God.' This link between fellowship and finance is demonstrated at Pentecost when the newborn church expressed its 'fellowship' (*koinōnia*; Acts 2:42) by having all things in common (verse 45); *i.e.* all who had capital realized and distributed it as income among the fellowship according to need (4:34f.)—the primitive Christian communism which was a guiding light to early Marxist thought.[8] Nor may we forget the Old Testament teaching which no doubt lies behind this New Testament witness (cf. Gn. 14:20; Lv. 27:30; Nu. 18:21f.; Dt. 12:6f.; 1 Ch. 29:6f.; Ezr. 1:6; 2:69; Ne. 10:32f. and Mal. 3:10).

One of the most significant instances of the relationship between fellowship and finance is the matter of Paul's collection.[9] This was a collection which Paul took up from the Gentile churches which he had founded under God, the money to go to help the churches of the Hebrews in the Jerusalem area which were suffering acute poverty and famine (cf. Rom. 15:25f.; 1 Cor. 16:1f.; 2 Cor. 8 and 9). It was probably first suggested at the Council of Jerusalem in Acts 15 (Gal. 2:10).

This background, if the correct one, is very important since the purpose of the Council was to deal with the difference of viewpoint being expressed in the Gentile and Hebrew churches on the question of the law and circumcision in particular (Acts 15:1 and 5). The division was a potentially dangerous one, though its importance has been greatly over-stressed in some recent New Testament criticism. In the situation of uneasy peace which developed after the Council—a peace made no easier by Paul's subsequent confrontation with Peter (Gal. 2:11ff.)—the collection for 'the poor among the saints at Jerusalem' came to assume a deeper significance. It was not simply an act of Christian charity but a symbol of the essential unity of both groups in the one Lord Jesus Christ. Thus the collection became an expression of fellowship and this explains the tremendous significance with which Paul invested it (cf. Rom. 15:27; 1 Cor. 16:2; 2 Cor. 8:1—9:15). 'The collection was in its origin a symbolic gesture declaring the new fellowship between Jew and Gentile in Christ . . . it was the outward pledge of an inward unity which was as yet perilously fragile.'[10] Paul even goes so far as actually to describe the collection as *koinōnia* in 2 Corinthians 9:13 and Rom. 15:26 (cf. Heb. 13:16). Paul refers to the gifts of the Philippians in the same exalted language in Philippians 4:15 where he speaks of a 'partnership *(koinōnia)* . . . in giving and receiving'.[11]

The message of all this ought to be clear enough. The New

Testament regards sacrificial financial giving to our fellow Christians as an indispensable expression of love and as an act of fellowship in which fellowship is both demonstrated and deepened. How do we stand in the light of this? Perhaps we need to take our Sunday offerings out of the clouds of exalted phraseology with which we tend to surround them ('the Lord's offering', 'our continuing worship', *etc.*) and to see them quite coldly (but not unscripturally) as what we are prepared to give to each other; *i.e.* as an index of our concern for the fellowship of our church. And if that only amounts to a couple of 10p pieces a week for wage-earners then let's stop all our pious cant about not finding fellowship in our church! This applies equally, of course, to all our giving to the church. Does a real blockage of fellowship not lie just here in many cases? Sacrificial giving has a great way of warming the heart. Perhaps it would do us good to see our missionary giving in this way at times; as a straightforward expression of our feeling for our brothers and sisters in Christ in the churches of Brazil, Africa, India, *etc.*, and an expression of our unity and fellowship with them. Certainly there are some parallels here to Paul's collection for the Hebrew churches. Be that as it may, the brother who is reputed to have requested that his wallet be baptized along with him surely had the Bible on his side. As Helmut Thielicke has put it, 'Our pocketbooks have more to do with heaven and also with hell than our hymn-books.'[12]

If we love the people of God then we will be openhanded towards them. Meagre giving to the people of God both in our own local fellowship and those in other lands is a denial of love and a serious breach of fellowship. Our faith is empty unless it is expressed in works of love. We cannot belong to the people of God and be indifferent to the tremendous need both in this country and overseas for finance on as large a scale as we can afford to give it. Experience certainly confirms Paul's view which we noted above: money does cement relationship. How often have Christians discovered, as if for the first time, the reality of the love of their brethren when they have passed through a difficult time financially and proved in a practical way how real was the love of their fellow believers? Such an experience of love in practice is something which is not readily forgotten, but which goes on enriching and deepening the relationships of God's people for years to come.

Here then are six ways in which love expressed itself among the first generation of Christians. All of these avenues are still open to us. But these six do not exhaust the possibilities. They merely give examples of what real love is like. It is not a matter simply of words and talk but it will always 'show itself in action' in ways like these.

1. L. Morris, *op. cit.*, p. 177, who comments, '*Merimnaō*, the word for "*care*", often has the notion of anxiety. It is a strong term, and denotes no tepid emotion.'
2. P. Tournier, *A Place for You* (SCM, 1968), p. 170.
3. J. Philip, *op. cit.*, p. 66.
4. B. Larson, *Dare to Live Now!* (Zondervan, 1965), p. 110, cited by J. R. W. Stott, *One Body* (Falcon, 1969), p. 70.
5. J. R. W. Stott, *op. cit.*, pp. 81–91.
6. K. Miller, *A Taste of New Wine* (Word Books, 1963).
7. On the use of the home for evangelism see M. Warde, *Take My Home* (Scripture Union, 1969); R. Capenerhurst, *You in Your Small Corner* (IVP, 1967).
8. F. Engels, 'On the History of Early Christianity', in Feuer (ed.), *Marx and Engels* (Anchor Books, 1959), p. 168ff.
9. See K. Nickle, *The Collection: A Study in Paul's Strategy* (SCM, 1966).
10. L. S. Thornton, *The Common Life in the Body of Christ* (Dacre Press, 1942), p. 9.
11. A. R. George, *op. cit.*, p. 182.
12. H. Thielicke, *The Waiting Father* (James Clark, 1964), p. 103.

8

Fellowship in the gospel

In earlier chapters we have identified the basis of Christian fellowship as being a common participation in the life of God. At one or two points, however, the New Testament refers to this basis in another way. It speaks of a fellowship 'in the gospel'.

This phrase occurs in Philippians 1:5 where the probable meaning is of a fellowship *(koinōnia)* in making the gospel known. In 1 Corinthians 9:23 the idea recurs with a somewhat different sense. The apostle Paul speaks here of adapting his evangelistic approach to the various groups he sought to reach (19–22) and claims justification for his flexibility in terms of 'the sake of the gospel', and adds 'that I may share in its blessings' (23). The 'blessings' which Paul hopes to share are 'the blessings of salvation which (the gospel) promises.'[1] To participate in Christ, then, can equally well be described as participating in the gospel and its benefits. 'The gospel and the blessings which flow from it are here (1 Cor. 9:23) regarded as something in which all Christians have a share.'[2] Christian fellowship is fellowship on the basis of the gospel. The gospel is the door of entry to the fellowship of Christ and his people.

A common basis of truth

This fact has an important implication. Since Christian fellowship is constituted on the basis of a response to truth, it continues to be effective only on that basis. The gospel makes certain quite specific assertions. It makes reference to God's claim upon our lives and our failure to repond to these claims, *i.e.* our sin (1 Cor. 15:3; Eph. 2:1ff.; Rom. 1:17—3:19). It refers to God's gracious response to our need in Jesus Christ, and his death for us on the cross (Acts 2:32; 10:39; 13:28f.; 1 Cor. 1:23; Rom. 3:25; *etc.*). It refers to our receiving forgiveness and new life through repentance from our sin and our faith in Christ crucified and risen (Acts 2:38; 10:43; 13:38f.; Eph. 2:4-10; Rom. 10:9; *etc.*). These truths are the essence of the gospel. To depart from them is to move away from the basis of fellowship, and indeed, to depart from Christ himself.

Thus the fellowship we share in Christ is not a nebulous kind of business based simply in a commonly-claimed experience and sustained only insofar as we are able to maintain the reality of that experience. Fellowship has a truth content. The early Christians are described as devoting themselves to 'the apostles' teaching and fellowship' (Acts 2:42). Right at the heart of their new experience of oneness was the teaching ministry of the apostles. Acts 6 represents the apostles in this first period of the church as devoted 'to the ministry of the word' (Acts 6:4). It was a church centred on God's Word, which for them meant the Old Testament Scriptures which they now saw fulfilled in the ministry of Jesus, and the word of the apostolic teaching based upon the instruction and teaching of Jesus. It was in such a community and among men and women for whom these things were central that the Holy Spirit gave the gift of fellowship. Fellowship is only possible on the basis of the apostolic gospel. Where this is denied then fellowship 'in the gospel' is excluded from the outset.

This truth has been rediscovered in recent years. In their enthusiasm to find unity among professing Christians some ecumenical addicts attempt to find the lowest common denominator of commonly-held conviction and seek on that basis to achieve a unity which is strong and effective. In practice the results are frequently meagre in the extreme. But this is entirely what we should expect in the light of the New Testament link between fellowship and truth. It is only on the basis of a full-hearted commitment to the revealed truths of apostolic Christianity that fellowship is conceived. To reduce this basis or modify it to meet contemporary tastes and ideas is in effect to cut the ground from under one's feet. When church groups are brought together on such a basis there is no depth of foundation upon which to build and not surprisingly the degree of real commitment which subsequently expresses itself is correspondingly minimal. Only the truths of apostolic Christianity, embraced and whole-heartedly adhered to, effectively break up the sinful isolation of the human heart and create the possibility of true relationship at depth with others. All schemes of unity which soft-pedal truth are therefore condemned to failure before they even begin. They may attain a formal kind of union in which people go through the motions and act in a relatively co-ordinated manner; but such schemes cannot by the nature of the case produce that depth of commitment and that sense of ultimate loyalty which the New Testament refers to as Christian fellowship. Truth and fellowship belong together and the one cannot be had without the other.

Partnership in spreading the gospel

However, a second way in which 'fellowship' and 'the gospel' are linked in the Bible is the aspect which is in view in Philippians 1:5. Here Paul thanks God for the Philippians' 'partnership *(koinōnia)* in the gospel'. There is some uncertainty how exactly to translate these words as Paul's construction here is an unusual one. But a good case can be made for the translation implying 'your partnership/fellowship in furtherance of the gospel'.[3] Paul and the Philippians had shared together in the spread of the gospel and for this Paul is thankful to God. The apostle may well have in view the Philippians' financial support of their 'missionary' apostle in the Gentile world. One way or another they had made a significant contribution to the evangelistic work Paul was engaged in and hence had been his partners or 'fellowshippers' in it.

Fellowship then does not simply imply an inward look towards the relationships which exist between the members of the Christian community. It also implies an outward look towards the non-Christian community. Our fellowship with one another is intended in the purpose of God to represent the platform from which the gospel can be preached to the world.

An instance of the term *koinōnia* which points in a similar direction occurs in Luke's account of Jesus' call of his disciples, which was referred to earlier. Simon Peter and his friends are described as 'partners' *(koinōnoi)*, implying that they were joint-owners of the fishing business (Lk. 5:10 and 7). Jesus then uses their business partnership to convey the terms of his call to them and of the work they were to do in the kingdom: 'Henceforth you will be catching men' (verse 10). They are now to be partners in the business of winning men and women to the kingdom. Paul's description of Titus in 2 Corinthians 8:23, 'my partner *(koinōnos)* and fellow worker in your service', has similar implications.[4]

The biblical evidence for this aspect of the link between 'the gospel' and 'fellowship', however, need not be confined to the usage of the word *koinōnia*. There is another vivid illustration of it in Philippians. Paul describes the Christians there as 'striving side by side for the faith of the gospel' (1:27). This is an allusion to the gladiatorial contests which were a regular feature of life in the Roman colony of Philippi (1:27 and 30). Sometimes a group of gladiators would be forced to fight in a team either against another group, or against some wild beast or beasts. In such a situation unity and partnership were necessary for survival. The Philippians are engaged together in a similar battle for the spread of the gospel, and the effectiveness of their witness to, and defence of, the gospel is bound up with the depth of their fellowship, *i.e.* their ability to support one another and stand firm together for the truth.

Perhaps the clearest and most challenging reference of all is the words of Jesus in John 13:35f.: 'By this all men will know that you are my disciples, if you have love for one another.' We should probably link with this reference words from Jesus' high-priestly prayer in John 17. He prays that his disciples 'may all be one; even as thou, Father, art in me, and I in thee, . . . that the world may believe that thou hast sent me' (verse 21). This latter reference is frequently used in the context of ecumenical overtures, but in fact its primary reference was to a small, visible company of disciples, and there would appear good reason for retaining that as its primary reference. It is to be referred therefore, in the first instance, to relationships in the immediate context of the local Christian group. In both these passages Jesus binds inward fellowship and outward witness indissolubly together. What we are in our relationships with one another will be what we will reflect in our witness to the world. It is impossible to be one thing in our fellowship and another thing in our witness. The quality of our relationships within the church will determine the effectiveness of our witness outside the church.

The power of a loving community

Jesus is prepared to base the evidence of the truth of the message which the church proclaims upon the quality of the relationships between its members. Here is the mark by which the church will be recognized in the world and be known as the people of Christ, by its love. We explored in the fourth chapter the meaning of love. Here we note the evangelistic implications. Here is Jesus' own prescription for effective communication. Here is the way in which the church can in every situation give proof to the world of its reality as the community of the risen Lord: by its love. Christian love is therefore what Francis Schaeffer has called 'the final apologetic'.[5]

In this day when much is written about the problems of communication it may be high time we came back to these words of Jesus in all their simplicity and devastating challenge. Perhaps it is their very challenge which causes us to ignore them. It is after all much less demanding to write a book on communication (or fellowship!), or give a series of talks on blockages to effective evangelism, than to live in love with my Christian neighbours in the local church. Perhaps until that price is paid we will be committed to endless frustration at this point. How we need to learn again the evangelistic power of a loving community.

This truth is particularly relevant in today's climate, as we pointed out in the first chapter. We live in a world which is dying for lack of true community. How attractive and persuasive in such a world will be the demonstration of love in action in a group of Christians who know in experience that 'God's love has been poured into our hearts through the Holy Spirit' (Rom. 5:5).

And if this love is flowing between the members of the church it will obviously flow out beyond it into the lives of the needy men and women around us with whom the church is constantly being brought into contact. Love is the universal language. Whatever the non-Christian may or may not understand about the gospel we preach he can certainly understand the attitudes with which we approach him. And there are few who can indefinitely resist the appeal of love.

It will be a terrible indictment of our local church if on the judgment day we stand condemned, not of a failure to try and reach men and women with our message, but of failing really to love them for Christ's sake, and for their own. It is a terrible possibility in Christian evangelism to rest content with telling people that *God* loves them as a substitute for the infinitely more costly, but also infinitely more Christian, business of loving them ourselves. True Christian evangelism has of course always recognized the need for both of these. Indeed if we truly love our neighbour we will long above all for them that they should hear the gospel and be saved. But a loveless evangelism is a fearful travesty from which every Christian church and every Christian witness should pray to be delivered.

Let there be no illusion at this point. Love of this kind *is* supremely costly. John's aphorism about love not being a matter of words and talk but being practical and showing itself in action (1 Jn. 3:18, NEB) is as applicable to love for those outside the church as to love for those within it.

Sometimes when we meet each other and exchange greetings with the familiar 'How are you?' and get the customary, breezy 'Fine, thanks', the answer is not quite as worthy as it appears. Perhaps it would be more to our credit and say more of the presence of the love of God in our lives if we were to have to concede more frequently that things weren't 'fine, thanks' but were pretty tough going, for the quite specific reason that we have really got involved with the problems and needs of some of the families round our doors, or because we have been constrained to accept responsibility in some way for some of the human casualties in our local community.

It is certainly nothing short of astonishing how many Christians seem able to pass unscarred through a world and society as broken and bleeding as our own with a happy smile on our faces and no lines of anxiety to wrinkle our shining brows. Such a pleasing image may gain us a high place in the estimate of our Christian friends, but it leaves us looking so terribly unlike Jesus, the man of sorrows who was acquainted with grief, and who learned obedience through the things he suffered, who was moved with compassion when he saw human need and who wept over impenitent Jerusalem. Jesus got involved at the price of a cross; how can it be that there is so little of his cross about our living? To love means to be vulnerable; it means accepting responsibility; it means giving ourselves away. Is this perhaps the reason why we are so uninvolved with human need so much of the time—our refusal to take up the cross? Do we not all have to confess to a selfishness which clings to its rights, to our material affluence, to our hoarded leisure-time, to our family privacy, to our right to order our lives for ourselves, and which resists having our lives shaken up and disordered by the unpredictable and demanding responsibility of really caring for others in need?

Obviously we are generalizing here. Many Christians *do* care and *are* involved; and obviously many of the things mentioned above are legitimate in their place. But we need to be so very sensitive about the way in which we can move from the position of thanking God for them, accepting our steward-ship of them, and assuring the Lord that we recognize them all as his gifts to be used in his service, to the position where they are *ours*, to hold on to, and defend, and maintain even in the face of blatant human need around us.

The challenge of this is inescapable, even if the implementing of it must be an individual matter as the Lord shows each of us what our particular responsibility is. But such is the way of love and it is in such sacrificial, caring ministry that we give witness to the reality of our faith (Jn. 13:34f.), and even perhaps meet up with the Lord himself (Mt. 25:31–46).

It is no accident that the love of God expressed itself in mission as John 3:16 reminds us. Love cannot be hoarded up; its very nature is to reach out and share. Such is true pre-eminently of the love of God which is the gift of the Holy Spirit in the fellowship of God's people. It will constantly find itself moving out to the world. The love of God is always a missionary love, whether in God himself or in his people. That is why the account of the coming of that love through the Spirit at Pentecost and the new fellowship to which it gave such glorious birth is set in the Acts of the Apostles, a book whose central theme is the spread of the gospel in accordance with the table of contents in 1:8, from Jerusalem to Judea, to Samaria, to the heart of the empire and the end of the earth. To be possessed of the love of God through the Spirit, be gathered into the living fellowship of his people, is to come under the compulsion of the ongoing mission of Jesus to the world. The promise of his presence, 'I am with you always', is set clearly in the context of the great commission to take the gospel of God to the world (Mt. 28:18ff.). Christ promises us his presence in a special sense when we seek to carry his commission into effect. It is where the church pushes out the frontiers of the kingdom that it is uniquely assured of the presence of its Lord. Conversely if we refuse the implications of his commission and try to shut him up in our cosy fellowship, we will lose something of his reality from our midst. Fellowship with him is also a 'fellowship in the gospel'. It is as we are committed and involved through witness, prayer, giving and caring in the ongoing mission of Christ to the world that we will, like Paul, be able to witness to the wonder of his presence, and it is as we commit ourselves corporately to his mission that our fellowship with one another will attain more closely to the pattern of his will.

1. G. Kittel (ed.), *Theological Dictionary of the New Testament*, III (Eerdmans, 1966), p. 804.
2. L. S. Thornton, *op. cit.*, p. 32.
3. *Ibid.*, A. R. George, *op. cit.*, p. 182.
4. *Cf.* J. R. W. Stott, *op. cit.*, pp. 76–77.
5. F. A. Schaeffer, *The Church at the End of the Twentieth Century* (Norfolk Press, 1970), p. 168, and *passim.*

9

Fellowship: some New Testament case studies

In the wisdom of God we are given in the New Testament not just theoretical principles by which to guide our lives. The word of principle becomes flesh before our eyes in the life of the first generation of Christian disciples, and we are allowed to see from their successes and failures something of how to put the theory into practice. This is very clearly the case as far as fellowship is concerned. We have discussed some of the theoretical and practical principles. Now we turn to several highly salutary case histories. We are introduced to several of the early churches through the letters written to them, and to their problems of fellowship, and in the way the apostles tackled their difficulties we get a very significant further dimension to the New Testament teaching on fellowship.

We will examine three of the churches, those at Corinth, Galatia and Philippi. We could have extended the list to others for the fact is that breaches of fellowship were just about the commonest problem faced in the early days of Christianity. Nor should that really surprise us if we reflect on the magnitude of the problems which faced the early Christian communities. As Principal Rainy once observed:

'Consider the case of these early converts. What varieties of training had formed their characters; what prejudices of diverse races and religions continued to activate their minds. Consider also what a world of new truths had burst upon them. It is impossible they could at once take in all these in their just proportions ... In addition to theory, practice opened a field of easy divergence. Church life had to be developed and Church work had to be done. Rules and precedents were lacking. Everything had to be planned and built from the foundation ... If all these things are weighed, instead of being surprised at the rise of difficulties we may rather wonder that interminable disagreement was averted.'[1]

In illustration of this, one need but reflect upon Acts 16:11–40 with its account of the conversion of three of the founder members of the church at Philippi; a leading business woman, a former slave-girl medium and the governor of a Roman prison. A more diverse trio it is difficult to imagine!

The church at Corinth

Paul, who had earlier been used to found the church (Acts 18:1–18) wrote 1 Corinthians to deal with a number of problems concerning which the Corinthians had written for advice (1 Cor. 7:1; 8:1) or concerning which he had been informed by others (1 Cor. 1:11; 5:1). The first of these was a problem of fellowship. Paul gives the whole opening section to dealing with it (1 Cor. 1:10—4:21). We will attempt to define the problem, see how it relates to our church situation today, and then look briefly at the stages of Paul's treatment.

The Corinthian church had apparently become divided into parties or groups (*schismata*, 1:10)[2] gathered round certain names, Paul, Apollos, Cephas (Peter) and Christ (1:12). There has been considerable discussion as to what exactly these names implied. The interpretation which most readily commends itself is that the 'Paul party' consisted of Paul's Gentile converts; the 'Peter party' would possibly be made up of converts from Judaism who took as their champion the apostle of the circumcision (Gal. 2:9); the 'Apollos party' were advocates of the Jew from Alexandria whose city was renowned for its literary culture and eloquence (Acts 18:24). It probably drew together the better educated, more sophisticated members of the Corinthian church. The 'Christ party' has had various interpretations of which one of the most recent is that it consisted of the 'spirituals' or 'enthusiasts' who claimed not to require apostles in any sense but to have direct access to Christ.[3] It is important to stress here that the divisions which existed were not on account of any important doctrinal disagreement as between Paul and the others. The author of Galatians could hardly have been so accommodating to Apollos and Peter in the ensuing argument had that been the case. There was agreement on the essentials of the faith; the divisions lay at a different level. Some have seen them as arising simply from different preaching styles, which view has some plausibility if Peter had also visited Corinth. But this is probably narrowing the issue over much. Paul, Apollos and Peter each represented a fairly distinctive approach to the Christian life in general: Paul the fiery evangelist/church-planter, Peter the more pragmatic, Palestine-orientated senior apostle, Apollos the cultured scholar/preacher. The result was the emergence of groups within the congregation claiming special allegiance to each and in the process constituting a serious threat to the fellowship of this local church.

This particular kind of party spirit has plagued the church though the ages and is as real a danger today as it ever was. The psychological and sociological factors involved in this kind of identification with particular names is complex.

'They can vary all the way from infantile dependence upon a parental substitute to a superstitious veneration for a holy man. In general they represent what has been commonly described as hero worship, but their complexity transcends this well-known category. Always there is a continuity of self-interest between the devotee and the idolised person with the latter in some respects the extension or enlargement of the psyche of the former.'[4]

Whenever a minister, preacher, theologian, evangelist, deacon or other church figure becomes a rallying point for dissension from our fellow church members, the focus for some form of 'inner ring' in our congregation,[5] then we are aligning ourselves with the Corinthians and stand in need of Paul's correction.

The apostle's full treatment of the problem runs through the first four chapters. For our purposes it will be sufficient to direct attention to the main thrust of Paul's teaching. He believes that mistaken thinking lies at the root of the Corinthian party divisions and he attempts to point them to a new and correct view of three realities.

(i) Jesus Christ (1:13). Paul as ever begins with Christ. He put three questions to them which in effect reduce to one: 'Have you thought what this state of affairs means to the Lord?' The Corinthians had been so concerned with their particular champion that they had never reflected seriously on how their behaviour related to Christ himself. They had acted as if there was an area of Christian life which he did not need to be brought into and which did not require to be submitted to his control and judgment. They could have their little parties, champions and squabbles, and he would smile tolerantly and be unaffected. 'What nonsense', says Paul. 'Don't you see that this sort of behaviour in fact is like rending the body of Christ in pieces, and don't you see you are giving to mere men the place of Christ in the work of salvation?' The Corinthians, and we today no less, were required to see what their baptism into the one Christ implied, viz. that we now belong together in the one body of Christ in our fellowship (1 Cor. 12:13) and that division is nothing less than the insane, impossible attempt to deny that reality and the unity which it embodies. As Calvin put it, 'If Christ is divided, who bleeds?' The application to ourselves needs no elaboration.

(ii) Themselves (1:18–2:16). At first sight this section appears to introduce a new subject altogether, the relationship between the gospel and 'worldly wisdom'. Paul, however, has not lost sight of his main objective. There is a very profound

relationship between this section and the party spirit in Corinth. Paul shows here that God in his approach to man has taken a humble road. The gospel he commissioned is folly to the wise men of the world (1:18–25); the Christians whom he has called to salvation are on the whole contemptible (1:26–31); the preacher he used was thoroughly unattractive (2:1–5); and the truth he disclosed was made known only by his own Spirit (2:6–16). But all this was no accident. It had the crucial effect of humbling man's pride and self-esteem so that men might learn to glory in God alone (1:29–31). Now all this relates to the party spirit in that the latter derives ultimately from a failure really to allow ourselves to be humbled by God and to glory in him alone. When we have seen ourselves as those who are dependent on God's grace from start to finish for our standing before him, then, and not until then, are we delivered from the partisanship which is really a sign of our sinful self-esteem.[6] Whenever we find ourselves adopting a loyalty to a particular Christian which seriously harms our fellowship with others in our church then we need to face up to the question of whether this particular allegiance is in fact an expression of our pride.

(iii) Their leaders (3:5–4:21). As far as a proper understanding of Christian leaders is concerned, Paul makes at least three points in this section:

(a) **The essential work is God's alone.** Leaders are at best only servants (3:5–9). How foolish then to be concerned with them as if they were of any significance. The human workers are nothing (3:7). The only real Christian worker is the Lord himself. 'Paul will say nothing which will obscure the primacy of God and the insignificance of God's ministers.'[7]

(b) **The leaders' work *will* be assessed,** but it is God alone who will make the assessment (3:10–15; 4:1–5). By their party spirit the Corinthians were trying to anticipate the final judgment and to usurp the role of the divine Judge. But God has reserved judgment to himself. Paul even makes the remarkable statement that he does not accept his own judgment of his own work (4:3). What release from the wrong kind of strain it would bring if we could all live by that principle.[8] Paul has more than a hint here that God's judgment may well turn out to be rather different from ours. The people who really count in our church, the preachers who truly serve God's glory, may prove to be folks who never had the limelight here.

(c) All the leaders belong to all the church (3:21ff.). Rather than feeling a special loyalty to one man as against another, the Corinthians ought to realize that they all—Paul, Apollos, Peter—belong to all of them in the one body of Christ. By their party spirit they were in fact robbing themselves of spiritual blessing and depriving themselves of the other leaders whom they felt to be inferior in gift and approach.

We may conclude with Paul's appeal: 'I appeal to you, brethren, by the name of our Lord Jesus Christ, that all of you agree and that there be no dissensions among you, but that you be united in the same mind and the same judgment' (1 Cor. 1:10).

The churches of Galatia

Here the threat to fellowship arose from doctrinal deviation. It is over this issue that perhaps the sharpest and bitterest divisions among Christians have manifested themselves over the centuries, nor do some present portents give promise of less stormy seas ahead. It is therefore imperative that a book on fellowship should take account of this issue. In our consideration of it, however, we will continue to give primary consideration to fellowship in the immediate context of the local church.

Controversy has raged over the question of whether the churches Paul addresses here were the ones formed during his first missionary journey (Acts 13:13–14:25) and located in present-day Turkey, the so-called 'South Galatian theory'; or churches founded by the apostle on subsequent journeys to the north (Acts 16:6; 18:23), the so-called 'North Galatian theory'.[9] In practice, while the former view appears on balance to have more to commend it, the precise location of the churches addressed does not materially affect the lessons this letter has for us. In either case Paul had come to the area, preached the gospel of God's grace in Jesus Christ, and churches had been formed from those who believed. After Paul's visit, however (and Galatians 1:6 seems to imply quite soon after) the churches had been visited by teachers known as Judaizers who argued that circumcision was essential for Christians (Gal. 2:3 and 7f.; 3:3; 5:2f. and 6f.; 6:15; cf. Acts 15:1f.). Faith in Jesus as Messiah was not denied by them but they insisted that such faith had to be complemented by this Old Testament rite. The reference to observing special seasons in 4:10, and the wider allusions to the law in general (4:21; 5:4; 3:2f. and 21f.) may indicate that the Judaizers were teaching adherence to other Jewish practices in addition to circumcision. The latter appears to have been the main issue, however, and it is the point Paul concentrates upon. Numbers of the Galatians were clearly much impressed by this Judaistic teaching and the result was division in the churches (5:15).[10]

Paul repudiates this insistence on circumcision in the strongest possible terms (1:6–9). This was not merely a harmless addition to the gospel which rendered them more complete Christians. It was rather a virtual denial of the gospel. It was an attempt to 'turn the gospel upside down'.[11] Paul even goes as far as to pronounce a solemn anathema, a curse which meant excommunication from God's people and hence the forfeiture of salvation, upon any and all who perpetrated such a view whatever their credentials—human, apostolic, or even heavenly (1:8). The reason for this thunderous condemnation is that Paul saw in this insistence on circumcision the introduction of an alien principle into the gospel of grace. By the little leaven of circumcision the whole lump of the gospel of grace was transformed (5:9) and salvation became a matter of human activity (cf. 3:10–14; 5:1–12; 2:16 and 21). Thus man's sinful pride went unchallenged and the cross of Christ by-passed and dishonoured (2:20f.; 3:1; 5:4; 6:12 and 14), and in the last analysis rendered valueless (2:21; 5:2). Paul therefore calls upon the Galatians to renounce this teaching and, by clear implication, those who were perpetrating it, and to return to the gospel of grace which was God's only way of salvation—a way taught by divine revelation (1:11–17) and one with which all the apostles were in agreement (1:18–2:10).

The Galatian divisions and the apostolic correction have several significant implications for church fellowship today.

(i) The truth. Fellowship has a truth content, a doctrinal element. When this latter is radically threatened then fellowship in the New Testament sense becomes impossible (1:6–9). Acts 2:42 draws a similar relationship between the 'apostles' teaching' *(didachē)* and fellowship *(koinōnia)*. The early church was a fellowship 'constituted on the basis of the apostolic teaching'.[12] The common participation in Christ which is what we have earlier seen *koinōnia* to signify, implied a common participation in the truth of Christ. Putting this another way, to be regenerated by the one Holy Spirit (Ezk. 11:19; Jn. 3:3ff.; 2 Cor. 3:3; 2 Thes. 2:13; Tit. 3:5) implies from the Scriptures the renewal of men's minds and thought patterns as truly as it implies the renewal of their desires and behaviour patterns (Rom. 12:1; 1 Cor. 2:16; 2 Cor. 4:6; Eph. 4:2f.; 5:10 and 17; 1 Jn. 2:27; 3:24; 4:13; 5:7f.). It is therefore to be expected that those in whom the Spirit dwells will manifest that indwelling by confessing the truth which he has revealed (1 Cor. 2:9f.; 2 Peter 1:20; Mt. 22:43; Acts 4:25; 2 John 9), and to do this corporately in a common acknowledgment of this truth in the church fellowship.

Truth does matter. Indeed it is primary in the sense that the church exists only on the basis of the gospel. Anything which challenges or alters any basic element of the gospel is therefore intolerable and it is folly to imagine that fellowship that is true to the name Christian will continue to be possible on such a basis. From this point of view to tolerate denials of any of the major elements of the gospel is effectively to attack and assault the fellowship we seek with others, for it is to encourage factors which render true fellowship impossible. There are some issues where unambiguous and energetic opposition is the only alternative if fellowship is to remain a possibility.

(ii) The limits. It is obviously crucial, however, to go on to try and determine the limits within which Paul's teaching in Galatians 1 applies to our church life today. Three factors at least need to be borne in mind:

(a) The situation where fellowship is no longer possible, as in Galatians 1, is confined to issues which affect the very essence of the gospel. We are required to distinguish between these areas of truth which are primary, where the essence of the faith is at stake and where compromise would mean a denial of the very gospel itself; and those which are secondary, where difference of viewpoint must be allowed and where such differences ought not to infringe our fellowship in our church with the brother or brethren concerned. Truths of a primary nature are: the supreme authority of the Scriptures as God's Word written; the being of God as triune, Father, Son, Spirit, one God; the guilt of man through sin and his consequent inability to save himself; the true humanity and deity of Christ; salvation from sin through the death of Christ alone; the resurrection of Christ from the dead and his glorious return; the necessity for the Holy Spirit to bring sinners to new life. It is this class of primary truth which is in view in Galatians 1.[13]

(b) We need to observe further that it is the active propagation of these errors by the Judaizers which Paul speaks out against so strongly. It is worth contrasting his attitude to such active propagandists with his tone in 6:1f. where he deals with the case of a brother who is 'overtaken in any trespass'. This appears to refer to the situation where the Christian is taken unawares and falls into sin almost without realizing the full implications of his action. While the Judaizers' teaching is not directly mentioned at this point in the letter it is impossible not to see this as at least in the background. There would no doubt have been folk in the Galatian churches who had been 'overtaken' ('on a sudden impulse', NEB) by the Judaizers', teaching and perhaps gone as far as observing some of the practices of the law without really seeing the full implications of their actions.[14] Such people are to be 'restored' in a 'spirit of gentleness' (cf. 5:22; Mt. 11:29; 2 Cor. 10:1) and in the humility which is ever conscious of its proneness to fall (6:1b). It is this second situation which is the more common in our church life and it is a fair test of our fellowship whether we are able to 'hold' and eventually 'restore' the man, woman or young person who is passing through a similar period of agonizing struggle with conflicting viewpoints. To apply the Galatians 1 approach in such cases will normally have the effect of driving these folk from our midst for good and is a real failure of fellowship on our part. In these instances we need the spirit of 2 Timothy 2:24f.: 'The Lord's servant must not be quarrelsome but kindly to everyone, an apt teacher, forbearing, correcting ... with gentleness.'

(c) Paul is much too good a student of human nature to restrict his attack on the Judaizers to their theological teaching. He also brings their hidden motives into the open. He speaks of their 'making much of' the Galatians in order that the Galatians in turn may 'make much of them' (4:17). He refers to their desire to 'make a good showing in the flesh ... in order that they may not be persecuted for the cross of Christ ... (and) that they may glory in your flesh' (6:12–13). Their theological deviation was bound up with pride and self-seeking and their accompanying unwillingness to 'die' for Christ (cf. 4:14; 2:20; Lk. 9:23–26; 14:26f.; Jn. 12:24; Phil. 1:29; 2 Tim. 3:12; Heb. 13:13). There is a most important insight here. A man's views can never be separated from the man himself and his inner motives. To assert this is not for a moment to suggest that there is no such thing as an objective theological truth or that the establishing and defence of that truth are unimportant. It is however to see with the apostle that these other deeper issues have to be kept in mind. Thus the teenager's rejection of the family faith *may* be a temporary expression of a wider adolescent search for identity; the member who agrees with every theological trend in the name of tolerance *may* be influenced more than he realizes by an emotional inadequacy which hungers for acceptance; the brother who is an aggressive upholder of orthodoxy *may* be using his reputation as a champion of the truth as a platform for his own pride. Recognizing such hidden motives behind theological division may not bring the parties closer, witness Paul and the Judaizers, but they do help us to confront the real issues, and at the level of local church fellowship may often prevent unnecessary division.

(iii) One further point. While Paul does not shrink from denouncing the Judaizers, the bulk of his treatment of the heresy is by way of a positive exposition of the truth of the gospel which has been revealed to him (2:15–6:10). Here surely is a word to us. The surest way of promoting the truth and hence of deepening fellowship is to expound it, to release it, to set it forth and to allow its inherent truthfulness to make its own impact on the mind and conscience. One of Paul's favourite adjectives for true doctrine is 'sound', which literally means 'healthgiving', and this applies to its effect upon relationships between church members as surely as to anything. Churches where the truth of God is set forth positively and relevantly in all its height and depth are the least likely to be split asunder by theological disputation.

'Speaking the truth in love, we are to grow up in every way into him who is the head, into Christ' (Eph. 4:15).

The church at Philippi

Paul's relationship with the Philippians was a very close one. The purpose of his letter was in the first instance to acknowledge their generous gift to him in prison (4:10–18). On the whole the Philippians were a cause of deep thanksgiving to the apostle (1:3–9). The one blemish on their otherwise comparatively spotless record was a certain tendency to division which had come to Paul's notice. Before attempting as well as we can to uncover the nature of these divisions it is worth pausing to remark that the combination within a single church of vital spiritual life on the one hand and tensions in relationships on the other should not altogether surprise us. It is a combination which has frequently expressed itself throughout the church's history. Handley Moule draws attention to it in this way:

'It is a sad but undeniable fact of Christian history that the spirit of difference, dissension, antagonism, within the ranks of the believing is not least likely to be operative where there is a generally diffused life and vigour in the community. A state of spiritual chill or luke-warmness may even favour a certain exterior tranquility; for where the energies of conviction are absent there will be little energy for discussion and resistance in matters not merely secular. But where Christian life and thought, and the expression of it, are in power, there, unless the Church is particularly watchful, the enemy has his occasion to put in the seeds of the tares amidst the golden grain.'[15]

The aftermath of the Reformation and the Evangelical Revival of the seventeenth century spring to mind immediately as historical proof of this. The welcome flow of new life and zeal which some churches are experiencing at present should therefore put us on our guard in this respect, and serve to underline how relevant the New Testament teaching on fellowship, and the Philippian situation in particular, is.

The divisions at Philippi were apparently neither as pervasive as in Corinth nor as fundamental as in Galatia. They are more to be inferred from Paul's insistence on unity (1:27–2:16) than being spelled out explicitly. The clearest reference to actual division is 4:2–3 where Paul urges the reconciliation of two of the leading women workers in the church. There is also in 3:12–16 the hint of some kind of perfectionist wing in the fellowship who held views of the Christian life which Paul is quick to challenge. Another ingredient of disunity is possibly present in the reference in 1:14 to most of the brethren being made bold in their witness. Those who remained timid may well have felt alienated and 'judged' by their more forthright brethren and so tempted to react against them. In general however the situation at Philippi, as often in churches' experience, was not one of open conflict in the church but one where certain tendencies towards disunity were smouldering beneath the surface and constituting a potential danger to the fellowship.

Despite the fact that the threats to fellowship at Philippi were still only threats Paul treats them with great seriousness, which should serve as a reminder of how much lower our standards of fellowship often are than those of the New Testament. A major reason for Paul's taking such a serious view was the effect division had on the church's witness to the gospel. He refers to this both at the beginning (1:27) and at the end (2:14-16) of his section on unity. Paul uses a graphic picture to convey this. He likens the Philippians to a team of gladiators 'striving side by side for the faith of the gospel' (1:27).

This points to the very challenging implication which we noted in the last chapter that the effectiveness of our witness as a church is bound up in the closest way with the mutual relations of our members. A divided church is an ineffectual church. We owe it to the needy multitudes around our doors (to put it no higher) to live together in fellowship. One wonders if our comparative lack of impact upon our neighbourhood has often to be traced to this rather squalid source—our petty-minded divisiveness (Jn. 15:12; Rom. 13:8f.; Jas. 2:8; 1 Pet. 1:22; 1 Jn. 4:7f.; etc.).

Paul attempts to resolve this problem in two stages. Firstly he launches a personal appeal (2:1-4),[16] and then secondly he points to the example of the Lord Jesus Christ (2:5-11).

As to the former, Paul's appeal for unity on personal grounds, there are numerous problems of interpretation. 'If' in verse 1 could perhaps be rendered by 'since'. Paul is not raising hypotheses here. He is reminding them of four things they know to be true.

(1) *Paul's personal authority:* 'If there is any encouragement in Christ.' Paul has been appointed by Christ to encourage and exhort the Philippians. If this carries any weight with them they should obey his call to be at one.

(2) *The demands of love:* 'If . . . any incentive of love.' The love here may be their love for one another as Christians[17] or Christ's love for them.[18] Either way this lays obligation on them to be united.

(3) *Their common participation in the Holy Spirit:* 'If . . . any participation in the Spirit.' Unity is clearly implied by the fact that it is the same Holy Spirit who regenerated and now indwells each of them (1 Cor. 12:13; Eph. 2:18).

(4) *The affection and sympathy they claim to feel for Paul.* 'If . . . any affection and sympathy.' If their feelings for the apostle were as real as they claimed they should express this in acceding to his plea that they live together in real fellowship.

The application of these truths goes far beyond its first century context.

Paul is not done yet. Something deeper and higher remains to be said for the real root of the divisiveness has not yet been exposed. This root was pride (*cf.* 2:3 'selfishness' and 'conceit') and the answer to pride, and hence the key to real fellowship at Philippi, lay in a new spirit of humility among the members. In seeking to produce such a spirit, however, Paul is not in the position of a mere moralist urging bad people to be good ('Come on, you must be humble', *etc.*); he is a Christian apostle addressing a company of Christian people. This means two quite revolutionary things. Firstly, humility is not merely an abstract virtue, it is a Person. Humility has been incarnated in the life and death of the Lord Jesus Christ. Not an abstract quality of lowliness but the mind of Jesus was what Paul could appeal to (2:5–12). Secondly, this very Jesus was alive and in the midst of the Philippian fellowship. They were not thrown back upon their own resources. They already had his mind to some degree by virtue of their participation in Christ by the Spirit (2:5). Thus Paul in effect is simply summoning them to be what they are in Christ, to live out the reality of their existence in Jesus Christ.[19] The fellowship they needed to recover was in fact already theirs, for fellowship is simply the reality of the life of Jesus expressing itself among his people. This mind of Jesus had expressed itself in a refusal to stand on its dignity, to claim its prerogatives, to take its rightful place, to assure itself of its proper recognition, or all the other things that so often govern our attitudes to each other (2:6). Unlike Adam[20] who snatched at the lure of likeness to God (Gn. 3:5, 'you will be like God') Jesus, who was God from eternity (2:6a), renounced the privileges and rights of this status (2:7) and freely chose the way of humiliation in fulfilment of the Scriptures[21]—a humble stable in Bethlehem (2:7), a life of obedient dependence on the Father in Palestine (2:8), a death of unspeakable degradation outside Jerusalem (2:8b). *Such* was the mind of Jesus, and this is the mind we need; a mind which is the guarantee of true fellowship, and in default of which true fellowship will always be an impossibility. But this is the mind *we have* in Christ and hence the mind which ought to pervade and control the relationships in our churches. A church which is a stranger to humble service one of another after the pattern of Jesus is a church to which he is a stranger too. For ultimately the question of fellowship is not a question of who we are; it is a question of who Jesus Christ is. He is the living centre of our relationships and to let him be Lord of our lives (2:9–11), to set his Holy Spirit within us, to impart his humble character to us, is to find ourselves in loving fellowship with his other brethren.

The application of this is clear enough and Paul presses it home in 2:12–16. It is as we allow this mind to control our relationships that we will be able together to work out and express our salvation (2:12);[22] that we will attain the blamelessness and innocence which enable us to shine as lights in the world (2:15; *cf.* Mt. 5:16); and that we will be able to hold forth the Word of Life to this needy generation (2:16).

1. R. Rainy, *The Epistle to the Philippians* (Expositor's Bible, 1893), p. 82.

2. This word implies that no final separation had occurred. The parties still maintained an outward unity and continued to meet together for worship, *etc.*

3. T. W. Manson, *Studies in the Gospels and Epistles* (Manchester University Press, 1962), p. 207; F. F. Bruce, *I and II Corinthians* (*New Century Bible*, Oliphants, 1971), p. 33.

4. J. S. Glen, *Pastoral Problems in First Corinthians* (Epworth, 1965), p. 16.

5. *Cf.* C. S. Lewis, *Screwtape Proposes a Toast* (Fontana, 1965), pp. 28–40.

6. *Cf.* C. K. Barrett, 'To attach oneself devotedly to one minister is thus not a proper expression of Christian humility, but a denial of the sovereignty of Christ.' *The First Epistle to the Corinthians* (A. and C. Black, 1968), p. 95.

7. L. Morris, *op. cit.*, p. 66.

8. *Cf.* L. Morris, *op. cit.*, p. 75. '(A Christian's) own views on himself are as irrelevant as those of anybody else.'

9. For a full discussion see D. Guthrie, *Galatians* (*New Century Bible*, Oliphants, 1969), pp. 15–27; H. Ridderbos, *The Epistle of Paul to the Churches of Galatia* (Marshall, Morgan and Scott, 1953), pp. 22–35.

10. It is surely not accidental that Paul's list of the 'works of the flesh' in 5:20 includes enmity, strife, jealousy, dissension and party spirit.

11. J. Bligh, *Galatians* (St Paul Publications, 1969), p. 82.

12. F. F. Bruce, *The Book of Acts* (Marshall, Morgan and Scott, 1954), p. 79.

13. Paul's approach to the class of 'secondary' disputes may be gauged from his treatment of divergent views of the Lord's return in 1 Thes. 4:13–5:11; the Lord's Supper in 1 Cor. 11:20ff.; sanctification in Phil. 3:12–16; scruples about food and special days in Rom. 14:1ff.

14. 'Mistake rather than misdeed is the force', H. Ridderbos, *op. cit.*, p. 212.

15. H. C. G. Moule, *Philippian Studies* (Hodder and Stoughton, 1897), p. 88.

16. Commentators divide on whether Paul mentions these four things in order to create a considerate attitude to himself and his appeal or whether he was aiming directly at improving their mutual relations. The former is the view of the Greek Fathers and the prince of exegetes, John Calvin, see his *The Epistles of Paul to the Galatians, Ephesians, Philippians and Colossians* (St Andrew Press, 1965), p. 244. We follow this here. As an example of the latter view, see J. B. Lightfoot, *Saint Paul's Epistle to the Philippians* (Macmillan, 1913), p. 107.

17. So most commentators, *e.g.* Calvin, *op. cit.*, p. 244.

18. So Karl Barth, *Epistle to the Philippians* (SCM, 1962), p. 52.

19. *Cf.* J. Philip, *op. cit.*, p. 30f.

20. R. P. Martin, *The Epistle of Paul to the Philippians* (IVP, 1959), p. 92.

21. Taking 'servant' in 2:3 as a reference to the Suffering Servant of Is. 42:1f., *etc. Cf.* R. P. Martin, *op. cit.*, p. 100f.

22. *Cf.* J. Michael, *The Epistle to the Philippians* (Hodder and Stoughton, 1928), p. 98. 'Paul is not urging them as individuals to work at their personal salvation; he is urging the whole body of Christians at Philippi to work out their salvation as a community.'

10

Fellowship: the future prospects

In this final chapter we will turn our attention from the present to the future and consider what the Christian's experience of fellowship means when set in that perspective. This is not simply in order to conform to the normal story-book pattern and give the whole thing a warm, cosy 'they all lived happily ever after' sort of ending. To turn to the future is to respond to the clear testimony of the Bible.

One of the most important developments in Christian theology in our own period has been the recovery of an emphasis on the importance of future hope for New Testament Christianity, representing a welcome return to a clearly biblical emphasis. For whatever we may feel about it the early Christians were possessed of an unshakable conviction that their Lord, who had died and risen again, was returning in his glory to complete his work of redemption and to inaugurate a new and glorious order of things. This hope conditioned all of their beliefs and was a significant factor in every aspect of their lives. No exposition of Christian truth can afford to neglect this perspective. We therefore need to face the question as far as our present investigation is concerned what does all that we have seen about fellowship mean in the light of the fact of the Lord's return?

We will approach this from several angles.

The position of the church

The Bible's view of time is progressive. It moves forward from a definite beginning to a future goal. But this simple picture of a 'time line' needs one important qualification. The line is divided into two parts. History for the Jew was intersected and divided by the appearing of the Messiah and the coming of God's kingdom.

The roots of this idea lie deep in the Old Testament but it comes to fullest expression in the prophets. The hope was expressed of a new, future work of God which would deal once and for all with Israel's sin and would establish God's rule over the nations in an unambiguous manner. The instrument which God would use in this great new work of salvation would be his 'anointed one', or Messiah. The coming of the Messiah would be the centre of history. By bringing the new age of salvation into being he would be the fulcrum on which the whole of history would turn. Thus the 'time line' had two parts, or 'ages' as they were commonly called. There was on the one hand 'this present age', the age of sin and decay and disobedience, the period of time which ran from the creation and the fall right up to the appearing of the Messiah. On the other hand there was 'the age to come', the age of God's salvation, the so-called 'kingdom of God', which ran from the appearing of Messiah on into the eternal future.

In the fullness of time the Messiah appeared and the 'age to come', the 'kingdom of God', was brought into being. However (and everything depends upon this 'however'), the fulfilment was not quite in the manner which had been anticipated. For *the coming of the kingdom did not immediately destroy the old age of sin and decay*. Instead of one age simply giving place to the other, the two overlapped. The new age came in the ministry of Jesus the Messiah; but the old age continued, and will do so until his glorious return. Only then will the old age be truly destroyed and the life of the new age be fully manifest. Thus the simple picture of a line with two parts divided by a mid-point needs to be replaced by a line which implies that the second part runs for part of its length on top of the first part; *i.e.* that the two parts overlap one another for part of their course. This is the peculiar period 'between the ages' when the new age of salvation has come and yet the old age of sin still remains with us.

The church belongs to this period of overlap. It is called to bear witness to Christ and to live for him in the situation of tension created by the simultaneous presence of the two ages. This tension runs right through every Christian life. We know the pull of the two ages within ourselves. There is the old age, or 'old man' as Paul refers to it, which drags us down to sin and disobedience, and there is also the pull of the new age or 'new man', the Christian's essential being as a man regenerated by the Holy Spirit (*cf.* Rom. 7:14–25; Gal. 5:16–26; Col. 3:5–17; Eph. 4:22–24). In our struggle to live the Christian life we express precisely where we are in relation to God's purposes. We and all our fellow Christians are part of the overlap period. The church looks back to the mighty conquest of Jesus Christ in his death and resurrection by which the kingdom has come and the new age been inaugurated; it is conscious of the reality of the kingdom in its present experience of the risen Lord and the power of the Spirit; and it strains forward expectantly to that coming day when the victory won at the first Easter will be actualized for the whole creation (Rom. 8:18f.; 1 Cor. 15:24f.; Eph. 1:10f.; Phil. 2:10f.). The life of the Holy Spirit in the church is the life of the new age. In its experience of the Spirit the church is literally 'tasting the powers of the age to come' (Heb. 6:5; *cf.* 2 Cor. 1:22; 5:5; Eph. 1:13f.; 4:30; Rom. 8:16; Gal. 4:6).

The whole of this biblical teaching concerning the position of the church in the purposes of God has one important implication. It means that Christian experience here and now is an anticipation of the full life of the new age which will be realized when Christ returns and the old age of sin is finally destroyed. This fact brings to all Christian experience an element of forward-looking. All that we have and enjoy now drives us forward to what will be ours when the kingdom fully comes.

We can see from this perspective why the New Testament's preoccupation with the future is *not*, as was so often said in earlier generations, a sort of wish-fulfilment, a 'pie in the sky when you die' kind of thing. It arises directly from the central affirmations of the Christian faith. A Christianity which does not reflect an interest in and concern for the future, is a Christianity which has denied its biblical roots.

The fellowship between Christians is no exception to this. Our experience of fellowship here and now is a foretaste of the coming glory. It is a sort of first instalment of the glorious future fellowship of the redeemed. We are therefore required to interpret it in the light not only of what it can be here and now, but also in the light of what it will yet become. To miss this further aspect is to rob ourselves of a whole dimension. Christian fellowship by its very nature is a provisional thing; it is an anticipation of the perfect fellowship of the coming order. As a fruit of God's Spirit it is a manifestation of the presence of the kingdom, and as a fruit of God's Spirit it is at the same moment the foretaste, and therefore the guarantee, of the fellowship which awaits us on the further side of Christ's appearing (2 Cor. 1:22; 5:5; Eph. 1:13f.).

It is important in this connection to note how this accords with the Bible's teaching concerning the life which the people of God are to enjoy in the future. Obviously we are inevitably reduced to some extent to symbol and picture to depict that which by the nature of the case is beyond our present experience of things. However, it is impossible to miss the consistently *corporate* nature of the life to come in the various biblical passages which refer to it (Mt. 24:31; 8:11f.; 22:1f.; Rom. 8:17f.; 1 Cor. 15:23; Eph. 5:5; Phil. 3:20; Col. 3:4; 1 Thes. 4:16f.; Heb. 11:10; 13:14; 2 Pet. 3:13; Rev. 21:2–22:5; *cf.* also Is. 2:2f.; Ezk. 40–48; Dn. 7:13f.; Zp. 3:14f.; Zc. 14:5f.). Indeed the very fact that heaven is, in its final meaning, the full coming of the kingdom of God makes this point clearly. All thoughts of a lonely spiritual pilgrimage into the future in which we pursue an isolated, spiritual vision of God is really out of step with the Bible. The glory which is to be, if the biblical pictures have any validity at all, is an existence of rich and profound *community* in the common life of the glorified people of God. It will certainly be a corporate, social form of existence.

Thus our experience of fellowship here and now, superficial and fragile as it may often appear, is nevertheless of quite tremendous significance. It is the life of the 'age to come' in our present experience; it is the kingdom of God in the midst of time. And as such, for all its present limitations, it holds within it the unshakable promise of a fellowship which is yet to be, when our giving to one another will be unqualified, when our concern for one another will flow uninhibited, and when we shall love him, and each other, with unsinning heart.

New Testament hymns

In their examination of the text of the New Testament, scholars have uncovered in recent years a number of passages which from their content and literary form look very much as though they were early Christian hymns. Of course, like all exegetical tools, this one can be over-worked. One ought not to deny to the apostles in their letters the ability to cast their thought at times in lyrical forms without our having to trace it back to a number in the early church's 'Hymns, Ancient and Modern'!

There can be no doubt however that the early church was a singing church. It had the inheritance of the Old Testament psalter to get it on its way, and the psalms were soon supplemented by other 'hymns and spiritual songs' (*cf.* Eph. 5:19; Col. 3:16). It would therefore be much in line with what one would expect that the apostles should occasionally cite these, very much as a preacher will often do today in the course of a sermon (*cf.* Eph. 5:14; Phil. 2:5–11; 1 Tim. 3:16; Col. 1:15–20; Heb. 1:3; Rev. 15:3f.; *etc.*). In hymns such as these the early Christians gave expression to their fellowship by lifting voice together to the Lord in corporate praise. The hymns therefore give us a first-hand witness to the corporate fellowship of the early churches. It is significant that the hymns have a consistently future perspective (*cf.* Rev. 15:3f.; 4:8; 1 Tim. 3:16;

Phil. 2:10; Col. 1:15f.; Heb. 1:3). To have a share in the fellowship of the early church and to join in their praise and worship, was the foretaste of the glorious fellowship which will be experienced at the return of the Lord.

The sacraments

A similar link between Christian fellowship in the present and in the future is illustrated by the two gospel sacraments of baptism and the Lord's Supper. This is not accidental for, as Donald Baillie points out, the present time 'is a period in which we may say that the kingdom has come (since it came with the coming of Christ) and yet has still to come because the final consummation is not yet ... In this interim period the church is always looking back and looking forward. That is why the church needs sacraments. And in both baptism and the Lord's Supper the church looks both back to the death and resurrection of Christ, which have to be reproduced in us, and forward to the full enjoyment of the Kingdom ...'[1]

(a) Baptism

As far as baptism is concerned there is a clear link established between our fellowship in the present and the fuller fellowship of the glory to come. Baptism on the one hand directs us to the church since it is baptism into Christ and we cannot be baptized into him without being related to his body (1 Cor. 12:13; Gal. 3:27f.; Acts 2:41f.). Baptism therefore represents fellowship with the people of Christ. But on the other hand it also points forward since the Lord to whom it bears witness and with whom in faith it unites us is not simply the crucified and risen Lord of the first Easter; he is also the King who now reigns at the right hand of the Father and the Lord who is returning in glory at the close of the present age (Mt. 28:18ff.; Acts 2:33; 3:20f.; 8:37; 10:42; *etc.*). Thus baptism directs us forwards as well as outwards, to the coming of the King as well as the communion of his subjects. 'The day of baptism presses forward and calls for the day of the Lord.'[2]

But baptism confirms this perspective from another point

of view. To be a Christian means to be a believer in Christ. To be a believer in Christ implies more than believing certain things about him, *e.g.* that he was the son of God, *etc*. It means a living relationship with him. It means being united with him. Faith therefore, for the New Testament, means faith-union with Christ. But the Christ with whom we are united is the one who has died and risen again. Hence to be united with Christ means to be united with him in his death and resurrection (*cf.* Rom. 6:2–11; Col. 2:12f.; 2:20; 3:1–4; Gal. 2:20; 2 Tim. 2:11; *cf.* also chapter three above). The Christian is therefore one who has shared in some sense in the death and resurrection of Christ.

Now baptism is the God-given point where this faith-relationship with Christ is focused. Baptism points us to the death and resurrection of Christ where we died and rose again with him. It proclaims the amazing fact that for the Christian death is a thing of the past. Our funeral has already taken place and the grave lies behind us (2 Tim. 1:10; 2 Cor. 5:17; Jn. 11:25f.). They are all past history, away back BC. We now live AD in the endless year of our Lord, and all that lies before us is life, life, and more life (Jn. 3:16; 5:24; 6:50f.: 10:28; *etc.*). True, our bodies have still to be laid down in physical death. The present age of sin and decay still extorts is dues to this extent from us (2 Cor. 4:16—5:5; 1 Cor. 15:42–50). But that is not *death* in the full and terrible sense of the Scripture, death as the wages of sin (Gn. 2:17; Rom. 6:23). For us that is all a thing of the past and leaving it behind we stretch to life and glory. Such is the prospect which baptism holds before us.

(b) The Lord's Supper

The Lord's Supper proclaims the same pattern of truth, the same promise of fellowship. In an earlier chapter we sought to draw attention to the importance of the horizontal dimension of the Lord's Supper, the communion which we share with one another around his table. For the New Testament it is a fellowship meal in which our unity with our fellow believers is both expressed and strengthened (1 Cor. 11:17–30). But the future perspective is clearly present as well. It is explicitly referred to by Paul in 1 Corinthians 11:26 where he reminds us that we are to observe the ordinance 'until he comes'. Of similar import are our Lord's words preserved in Mark 14:25: 'Truly, I say to you, I shall not drink again of the fruit of the vine until that day when I drink it new in the kingdom of God' (cf. Lk. 22:18).

It seems clear that our Lord had in view here the Jewish picture of the heavenly messianic kingdom as inaugurated by a marriage supper (Mt. 8:11; 22:1–10; Lk. 13:29; 14:16–24; 22:29f.). Thus the sorrow of his impending sacrifice and parting is muted by the joyful expectation and promise of the coming of the kingdom. It is to be regretted that we have so largely lost sight of this future perspective to the Lord's Supper. Higgins makes just this point, viz. that the Lord's Supper 'is at one and the same time a remembrance of the death of Christ, and an expectation of perfect joy with him in the kingdom, which is already in a measure anticipated at each celebration by the experience of his risen living presence. There is no doubt that too often the first element, which is absolutely fundamental, has been allowed to exclude the other two, and that the modern church has largely lost that forward-looking expectancy and eschatological joy and hope which were characteristic of the early communities.'[3]

Interesting further testimony to the future perspective of the Supper in the early period is contained in the expression in 1 Corinthians 16:22, *maranatha*. This is an Aramaic phrase and the original language is preserved in the text which implies that the phrase was a liturgical formula readily understood by Paul's Greek-speaking readers (*abba* is a similar instance). Translated, the phrase means either 'Our Lord comes', *i.e.* a confession of faith; or 'Our Lord, come!', *i.e.* a prayer. The weight of probability inclines to the latter meaning, especially if we bear Revelation 22:20 in mind.[4] What is particularly interesting therefore is that the early church order known as *The Didache* uses this exact formula for a service preparing for the Lord's Supper. Such a setting for the prayer bears significant testimony to the early church's understanding of the Supper—

as a fellowship meal anticipating the blessed fellowship of the redeemed at the return of the Lord.

Conclusions

All these lines of evidence converge to point us forward to the glorious prospect of Christian fellowship. They bid us see the fellowship we share here as the foretaste and guarantee of the fuller fellowship which is yet to be.

We can observe four implications of this truth:

(*i*) If our fellowship now is the foretaste of the fellowship of the future age then it surely presents us with the sheer *wonder* of Christian fellowship. At its deepest this is simply the wonder of the sovereign mercy of God which has stooped to us in our helplessness and need and lifted us into the blessed company of the redeemed. And what a wonder this is, that in our relationships with one another in the church of God we are in direct touch with eternity. For in these relationships we indeed 'touch and handle things unseen' as the coming glory of God meets us in the face of our brother and sister in Christ.

(*ii*) The future prospect of fellowship also serves to underline the *seriousness* of our relationships to one another. In these relationships we are at a different level from all others, whether social, vocational or even, in a sense, family. These relationships in the body of Christ cannot be confined to merely physical situations or even to our mortal existence. Our relationships with one another in Christ have a transcendent perspective. Accordingly they must not be lightly treated or carelessly discarded.

(*iii*) The prospect of fellowship in the future also enables us to take account of the *limitations* of all our experience of fellowship in this life. The full giving of God to his people awaits the coming of the Lord. Thus our experience of fellowship now will always fall short of that. The old age of sin is still with us.

It inhibits our lives at every level. This is no ground for accepting low standards. Quite the contrary. But it is to reckon with the fact of limitation. Indeed to attempt to claim *too* much is really to make the mistake of rendering the return of the Lord unnecessary. No, our fellowship here will not attain to the dimensions of our fellowship there. But we need not despair on that account. The limitations of the present can be lived with, for they are not the whole story. They represent only the first, brief, preliminary preface. The 'whole story' has still to be told and the errors and inconsistencies of the preface can be put up with in anticipation of what has yet to be unfolded to us.

(*iv*) The prospect of future fellowship in the coming glory is also an aspect of the *joy* of Christian fellowship. This derives not so much from the guarantee it represents of our personal share in the glory ('. . . that will be glory for me', *etc.*) but rather in the promise it affords of the crowning and acknowledgment of our blessed Lord Jesus Christ.

'Oh the joy to see thee reigning,
Thee, my own beloved Lord!
Every tongue thy name confessing,
Worship, honour, glory, blessing,
Brought to thee with one accord;
Thee, my master and my friend,
Vindicated and enthroned,
Unto earth's remotest end,
Glorified, adored and owned!'

Finally such a prospect ought not to lead us to sit around in holy huddles awaiting the coming rapture totally unconcerned for the plight and suffering of multitudes of our fellow men and women. For all its 'hope of glory' the New Testament is utterly impatient with such an attitude which it sees as nothing less than a denial of the faith (*cf.* Mt. 25:14ff.; Lk. 19:12ff.; 2 Thes. 3:6ff.). Rather, for the New Testament it is precisely this heavenly perspective which is the driving inspiration to witness and service in this needy, broken world (1 Cor. 15:58; Mt. 28:18ff.; Mk. 16:19f.; 1 Thes. 5:8ff.; 2 Cor. 2:14f.; Phil. 3:20f.; 2 Pet. 3:11f.).

Nor is such inspiration to service confined to the New Testament. Let Lord Shaftesbury, the great evangelical social reformer of the nineteenth century, speak on behalf of a great line of witnesses when he testified, 'I do not think that in the last forty years I have lived one conscious hour that was not influenced by the thought of our Lord's return.' Service now, glory then, and 'what . . . God has joined together, let not man put asunder'. The two belong indissolubly together, for we go to men in their need as the servants by grace of the one who has come and is coming, and whose love shed abroad in our hearts is the guarantee of a coming day in which that love will overflow in unimaginable splendour and the whole creation, whether in joy or judgment, will own its Lord.

If we believe such things, then let us love and serve one another like those at Pentecost who 'devoted themselves to . . . fellowship' (Acts 2:42). And let us do it, not for our own sakes, or even simply for the good or glory of our local church, but ultimately for the best reason of all: the honour and glory of our blessed Lord and God. To him be the glory for ever and ever.

1. D. M. Baillie, *The Theology of the Sacraments* (Faber and Faber, 1957), p. 69f.
2. R. Schnackenberg, *Baptism in the Thought of St Paul* (Oxford, 1964), p. 199.
3. A. J. B. Higgins, *op. cit.*, p. 54.
4. O. Cullmann, *The Christology of the New Testament* (SCM, 1959), p. 208f.